Dressmaking with
Special Fabrics

Rosalie P. Giles

Dressmaking with special fabrics

MILLS & BOON LIMITED
LONDON · TORONTO · SYDNEY

First published 1976 by Mills & Boon Ltd
17–19 Foley Street, London W1A 1OR

Text and illustrations © 1976 by Rosalie P. Giles

Filmset by Keyspools Ltd, Golborne, Lancs
and printed in Great Britain
by A. Wheaton & Co., Exeter

ISBN 0 263 06253 8

Contents

Foreword

While this book will meet the needs of students working for GCE 'A' Level and City and Guilds, it can also be used by a much wider public. It has surely happened to all of us to be lured into buying some beautiful, unusual fabric, and then, on getting it home, to realise that making it up is not going to be as easy as we thought. In such a crisis, Rosalie Giles' crisp, clear advice is just what is wanted. For those who are deliberately adventurous in their dressmaking, it will be a useful guide enabling them to proceed with confidence.

Abbreviations

The following abbreviations are used throughout the book

R.S. = right side
W.S. = wrong side
mm = millimetre
cm = centimetre
m = metre

Measurements

Metrication is still causing some uncertainty. The Metrication Board has recommended 90, 120 and 140 cm as the metric equivalents for 36, 48 and 54-inch widths. Some leading pattern books, however, quote 115 instead of 120, while 150 (60 inches) is not uncommon. Also, the shops are still displaying yard-wide goods variously marked as 90, 91 and 92 cm.

Closer equivalents at 2·54 cm = 1 inch are

36 in = 91 cm
48 in = 122 cm
54 in = 137 cm

and these have been given in this book. Other (approximate) equivalents are also given, but readers who can get into the habit of "thinking metric" will be rewarded by finding the system very easy to manage in the long run.

1. Silks

There are many types of silk fabric. Some are more difficult to handle than others and as they are expensive and luxurious one cannot afford to make mistakes.

TYPES OF SILK FABRIC AND THEIR USES

Jap silk. A very lightweight fabric used mainly for linings and underlinings.

Taffeta. A lightweight fabric with a slight rib in the weave. Used for evening dresses and for linings.

Poult. Similar to taffeta but heavier, with a more pronounced rib. Used for evening dresses and bridal wear.

Douppion. Heavier than poult, with a distinct slub. Suitable for lightweight 'dressy' coats and suits.

Silk satin. A delicate type of fabric with a sheen. Used for lingerie. Heavier types are used for bridal wear.

Crêpe satin. A fabric in which both sides can be used. The top side has a pebbled surface with a sheen and the underside is smooth and matt. To give interest and texture inset parts of a garment such as decorative bands can be cut using the underside as the right side.

Silk brocade. A beautiful heavy fabric, sometimes really stiff. Used for evening dresses, wraps and wedding dresses.

Crêpe-de-chine. Made from twisted yarn and used for blouses and lingerie.

Organza. Stiffish and transparent. This is a sheer fabric used for dainty dresses and for evening and bridal wear.

Georgette. A soft sheer fabric with a crêpe-like surface, made from tightly twisted yarn. Used for evening dresses, blouses and négligés.

Chiffon. Similar to georgette but made from untwisted yarn so that it has a smoother, softer appearance. Used for evening wear, lingerie and blouses. For the treatment of georgette and chiffon refer to the chapter on sheer fabrics.

Surah or foulard. A soft lightweight fabric with a twill weave. Used for dresses, blouses, scarves, head-squares and ties.

Wild silk. Known as tussore, tussah or shantung. A fabric made from the silk produced by wild silk-worms. Originally a light beige in colour but it can be bleached and then dyed in other colours. Owing to the uneven thickness of the wild silk filament, this fabric has a characteristic slub throughout.

Velvet. Originally the pile of velvet was made from silk and it finger-marked badly. Nowadays most velvets are made from synthetic fibres which are much easier to handle.

Spun silk. A cheaper fabric made from fibres which are too short to produce higher-class fabrics. Used for dresses and blouses.

Silk jersey. Known as milanese fabric, a knitted, heavy, slippery fabric used for evening wear.

Silk fabrics in use today which present the most dressmaking problems are:
1. Chiffon and georgette, see chapter 15.
2. Velvet, see chapter 6.
3. Brocade.
4. Wild silk.
5. Silk jersey.

BROCADE

This fabric sometimes incorporates metal thread. On account of its expense there are substitutes today made from man-made fibres, but these can have the same making-up problems as silk brocade.

Width. 91 cm (36 in.) or wider.

Styles. Let the beauty of the fabric make the dress rather than elaborate complicated cut. Usually sculptured styles suit this fabric best.

Sewing thread. Pure sewing silk.

Hand-sewing needle. Sharps size 7 or 8.

Machine needle. Size 11 or 14 English or 70–80 Continental, depending on the weight of the fabric.

Machine stitch. 12 stitches per 2·5 cm (1 in.).

Interfacing. Organza or organdie.

Underlining & lining. Use jap silk for silk brocade and thin Tricel for rayon brocades.

Problems

1. The fabrics fray badly.
2. Real metal thread can scratch the skin.

Dealing with the Problems

1. Cut out with very sharp scissors, leaving a margin all round outside the pattern to allow for fraying.

   After cutting out, if a swing needle machine is available, work zig-zag stitch all round the cut edges to reduce fraying. If such a machine is not available, iron narrow strips of fusible fleece, e.g. Bondina, on the wrong side (W.S.) of the turning allowances and this will help to stick the fraying threads together.

   Seams can be neatened by machine zig-zag or by binding with crossway strips of jap silk.
2. Bind the seam turnings or use a loose lining.

Pressing

Press on the W.S. with a cool iron under a dry muslin cloth. Press seams over a roller and just the tip of the iron along the stitching line of the seam, to avoid an impression showing on the right side (R.S.).

Cleaning

Dry-clean only.

WILD SILK

Width. 91 cm (36 in.).

Sewing thread. Pure sewing silk.
Hand-sewing needle. Sharps size 8.
Machine needle. Size 11 English or 70 Continental.
Machine stitch. 12 per 2·5 cm (1 in.). Setting 2 on a Continental machine.
Interfacing. Must be very lightweight. Use organza or organdie.
Underlining & lining. If used jap silk is suitable.

Problems

1. Fabric frays.
2. Not always colour fast.
3. Fabric watermarks badly if pressed damp, leaving a permanent stain resembling a grease stain.
4. Seam turnings can leave shiny impressions on the R.S.
5. Perspiration rots the fabric.

Dealing with the Problems

1. Cut out with pinking shears leaving turnings wider than usual, so that the pinking can be trimmed off when turnings have to be neatened.
2. Test for colour fastness by wetting a small piece of fabric and pressing it dry between two layers of white muslin. If the colour stains the muslin the fabric should not be washed.
3. Press on the W.S. with a *cool* iron *completely dry*. Do not use a steam iron as incidental water spots coming from it can permanently spot the fabric.
4. Press all seams on the W.S. over a padded roller and then lift the turnings and press underneath them.
5. Always sew in dress shields.

Processes

Tailor tacking is inadvisable – partly because the threads would slip out of the fabric when it was handled and partly because withdrawing them after stitching could damage the delicate fibres.

Mark the fitting lines by tracing out with flat tacking.

When removing any tacking threads in the course of making up, always cut them into short lengths before withdrawing them so that they will not pull and drag the fabric.

Plain seams. The only satisfactory way to neaten the turnings is by hand-sewn overcasting which will give the flattest finish and so be less likely to leave an impression on the R.S. when pressed.

French seams should be used on blouses.

Hems. These can be difficult if dresses are not underlined. Fasten with slip hemming, see diagram. Level the hem and trim the turning to the required depth.

Fold the turning to the inside of the garment and tack through 6 mm ($\frac{1}{4}$ in.) up from the folded edge.

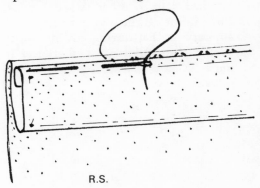

R.S.

11

Fold in the raw edge of the hem for 4–6 mm ($\frac{1}{8}$ in.–$\frac{1}{4}$ in.) and press lightly. Tack in position.

Slip hem by putting the needle in the folded edge and being careful to take up only *one* thread from the garment.

Remove all tacking and then press very lightly on the W.S. under dry muslin.

Cleaning

If the fabric is colourfast it can be washed by hand in warm soapy water. Rinse thoroughly and roll in a dry towel to remove surplus moisture. Hang up to dry.

Do not attempt to iron a garment until it is completely dry.

If the fabric is not colourfast it must be dry-cleaned, otherwise the colour will run in streaks.

SILK JERSEY

For general procedure refer to chapter 3 on Jersey Fabrics. However there are a few more points which apply more to this fabric than to other jersey fabrics.

1. This fabric is heavy, stretchy and slippery so that during cutting out it should be supported at all times. It must lie on a flat surface completely relaxed.

2. When silk jersey is cut out it should be cut approximately 12 mm ($\frac{1}{2}$ in.) shorter than the pattern and 12 mm ($\frac{1}{2}$ in.) wider to allow for the weight of the fabric causing it to drop and stretch lengthwise and reduce in width. It is wise to underline this fabric with jap silk cut to the exact size of the pattern in order to help the jersey fabric to retain its shape. Underlining will, of course, remove the elasticity of the jersey.

3. Fitting lines should be traced out with flat tacking to give greater accuracy.

4. Parts cut on the cross stretch greatly, therefore shoulder seams should be taped with fine ribbon or straight cut strips of jap silk which can be neatened in with the seam turnings.

To prevent neck and armholes stretching stay-stitch round them after cutting out. Stitch 6 mm ($\frac{1}{4}$ in.) wide strips of jap silk in with the facings or seams to prevent stretching during wear.

5. Hang the garment up overnight before levelling the hem so that it may drop to its full extent.

6. Use a cool iron and press under dry muslin very lightly on the W.S. Never press over tacking. Always press with the knitting rib and never across it, to avoid possible stretching. Press up and down only, never iron back and forth.

2. Crêpes

There are two types of crêpe material:

1. *Pure crêpe,* which is a fabric woven from yarn which has been highly twisted, this twist having been set in with moisture and heat. This gives the fabric a pebble-like or mossy surface and a great deal of elasticity. The yarn from which it is made may be silk, wool, cotton, rayon or synthetic fibre. The fabric is very fluid and drapes well but is rather difficult to handle, particularly the silky kinds which tend to slip about and stretch. It is not a fabric for the beginner.

2. *Moss crêpe,* which is fabric woven with untwisted yarn in such a way as to give it a matt crinkled appearance like crêpe. It is not elastic and apart from fraying it presents no difficulty to the dressmaker.

This chapter deals mainly with the problems of pure crêpe.

Width. Usually 91 cm (36 in.).

Uses. Blouses, dresses, very lightweight coats and suits.

Styles. The fluid nature of the fabric calls for styles with drapery such as cowl necklines which fall in supple folds, gathered and flared styles and even knife-pleated styles. Dresses cut on the cross give a sleek clinging effect. Try to avoid too many seams and inset pockets which may leave shiny impressions on the right side. Tailored styles are not suitable.

Threads to use. Pure sewing silk for silk, rayon or wool crêpes. 50 Sylko for cotton crêpes and synthetic thread for synthetic crêpes.

Linings. Underlining can be used to help the crêpe to keep a good shape but it must be chosen with great care because it must have the same soft draping properties that the crêpe has. Underline cotton crêpes with voile or lawn, wool, rayon and synthetic crêpes with jap silk or a very fine Tricel. Any heavier lining will cause the crêpe to wrinkle up on it.

Hand-sewing needle. Size 7 or 8 sharps.

Machine needle. Size 11 English or 70 Continental.

Machine stitch. Use a small stitch, about 14 per 2·5 cm (1 in.), or dial 1½ or 1¾ on continental machines. The stitch must be small to prevent the thread breaking when the strain is put on the seam in wear.

Problems

1. The fabric absorbs moisture readily and shrinks up.
2. The fabric is stretchy and slippery, making cutting out difficult.
3. The fabric frays badly when cut.
4. Impressions made by pins and tacking can be difficult to remove.
5. Shiny impressions are very easily made when pressing.

Dealing with the Problems

1. *Never* pre-shrink before cutting out.
   Press under a dry cloth with a steam iron. If the fabric is pre-shrunk it will reduce in size considerably and then in wear it will stretch out of shape and not relax back into its former size.
2. Pull a straight thread across one end of the fabric. Fold in half lengthwise, keeping the straightened end level, and pin the selvedges together down the whole length. If the fabric is folded over so that it is off grain it will form folds and rucks and will not lie flat, therefore it is important to get one end straight to ensure that it is folded on the grain.
   Always cut out on a *large* table and support the fabric so that it does not hang over the edge, for the full weight of it may cause it to stretch and lose width.
   Cut the crêpe 12 mm ($\frac{1}{2}$ in.) shorter than the underlining as it is inclined to drop and lengthen.
3. Cut out with pinking shears leaving wider turnings than usual so that they can be trimmed down later when they are neatened.
4. Do not tailor tack the crêpe but trace out the fitting lines onto the underlining fabric only.
   Never press heavily over any tacking.
5. Press seams on the W.S. over a roller, using the edge of the iron only. Place brown paper strips between the seam turnings and the garment before pressing. *Press* only and never run the iron along the fabric as this may cause it to stretch.

Processes

After cutting out (see above) place the underlining pattern pieces flat on the table and drop the crêpe pieces on top, coaxing them to fit the underlining exactly without any wrinkles. Baste-tack the two layers together with pure sewing silk as this will leave the least impression and never, never press over these tackings.

Seams. Tack all seams together with *small* stitches to prevent the sections slipping about on each other.

Plain seams may stretch when being made up, particularly when there is no underlining. To prevent this pin strips of tissue paper along the fitting lines,

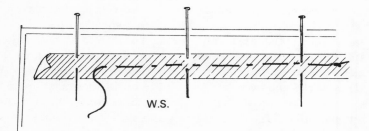

W.S.

making each strip the length of the seam as on the paper pattern. Pin the strip to the fabric across each end and then pin across at intervals, easing the fabric to fit the paper. Tack and stitch through all layers and then tear the paper away afterwards.

Stitch the seam with the paper underneath between the machine feed and the fabric to prevent the fabric being marked.

The seam is neatened by overcasting by hand or with a machine zig-zag. The hand-worked method gives the flattest finish and is less likely to leave a shiny impression on the R.S. when pressed.

Curved edges. Necks and armholes are liable to become stretched with handling and should be stay-stitched with a row of machine stitching just inside the fitting line, immediately after cutting out.

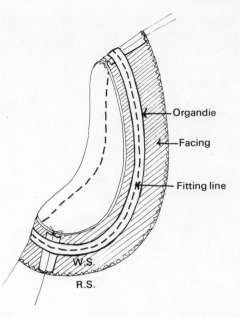

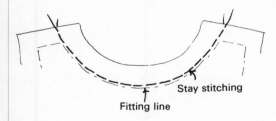

Alternatively, cut strips of organdie 6 mm ($\frac{1}{4}$ in.) wide and stitch them in with the facing along the fitting lines as shown in the diagram.

Buttonholes. Interline the buttonhole position with organdie to prevent stretch-

ing and work the buttonhole stitch over fine cord.

Rouleau loops and covered button moulds look very good on crêpe fabrics.

Hems. After levelling, overcast the raw edge of the hem and slip-stitch it in place to the underlining, being careful not to take the stitches through the crêpe.

Pressing

Press on the W.S. under a dry cloth, preferably with a steam iron. Do not let any moisture touch the fabric. Use a padded roller for pressing seams and put paper between the turnings and the garment. Remove all tacking before pressing the hem and avoid putting the iron

15

down on the folded edge of the hem; hold the iron just off the ironing cloth and let the steam press the edge. Then flatten the hem with a clapper (wooden block).

Cleaning

This fabric must be dry-cleaned.

Only moss crêpe can be washed with success.

All jersey fabrics are knitted and they can be made from any yarn — cotton, wool, silk, rayon, acetate and synthetic fibres such as nylon, Terylene, acrylics and Lurex. They are stretchy fabrics and comfortable to wear. Usually they stretch more across the width than down the length unless they are made from stretch yarn when they can stretch equally either way.

TYPES OF JERSEY FABRIC

These fabrics may be knitted in various ways:

1. *Single knits* which are really stocking stitch having one surface in plain knitting and the other side in purl stitch. Fabrics made in this way are cotton stockinette, nylon tricot and brushed nylon. Some single knits are constructed in such a way that they do not ladder, for example, cotton locknit.

   To give greater firmness single knits are sometimes bonded to a knitted backing. When buying this type of jersey fabric check it over very carefully to make sure that the 'grain' or lengthwise ribs of the knitting are running perfectly straight and have not been pulled awry by the bonding process, as this can ruin the finished appearance of a garment.

2. *Double knits*, which are worked on two sets of needles, are heavier fabrics and both sides look almost alike in plain fabrics. These fabrics are made in plain colours or they may have a pattern knitted into them. The latter are known as plated knits.
3. *Raschel knits* produce openwork lace-like patterns.
4. *Pile knits* such as stretch towelling are so constructed that the back resembles stocking stitch and the top surface has loops all over it to produce the pile. This fabric is made from stretch yarn. For information on this fabric see chapter 4.

Uses

1. *Single knits*. Lingerie, light-weight dresses, evening wear, linings, sheets and pillow cases.
2. *Double knits*. Day and evening dresses, light coats and suits and trouser suits.
3. *Raschel knits*. 'Dressy' dresses and blouses and bedjackets.
4. *Pile jersey*. Babies' clothes and beach wear.

Styles

1. *Single knits*. Choose soft easy styles, avoiding too much seaming as some of these fabrics tend to ladder.

2. *Bonded single knits.* More tailored styles are necessary for this kind of fabric owing to its greater thickness.
3. *Double knits.* Choose tailored styles and garments with top-stitched or saddle-stitched seams.
4. *Raschel knits.* Choose styles with few seams because of the lacy construction. Contrasting coloured underlinings can be attractive, showing through the open mesh of the fabric.
5. *Pile knits.* Choose easy styles without much seaming, which does not show up much in the pile.

Width. These fabrics vary much in width from 91 cm (36 in.) to 150 cm (60 in.) or even wider.

Sewing thread. This will depend on the fibre from which the fabric is made. Use mercerised cotton size 60 for cotton jersey, pure sewing silk for wool, silk and rayons and synthetic thread for synthetic fabrics such as crimplenes, nylons and acrylics.

Hand-sewing needle. Sharps, size 8.

Machine needle. The machine needle is very important and will vary with the twist in the yarn from which the fabric is made. Some needles have sharp points and others rounded ones which are specially suitable for some of these fabrics. When stitching a soft fabric where the yarn has a loose twist a fine, sharp-pointed needle size 11 English, 70 Continental, gives the best results as it will pierce the loose fabric cleanly without damaging the fibres. This type of needle is suitable for cotton, wool and silk jerseys.

Firmer fabrics made from tightly twisted yarns are best stitched with a needle with a more rounded point which will push the fibres apart and stitch between them. If this type of yarn were pierced by the needle it might be damaged and could ladder in wear.

Machine stitch. Use a small stitch – 14 per 2·5 cm (1 in.) or setting $1\frac{1}{2}$ on a Continental sewing machine. The thread is less likely to snap when strain is put upon it in wear if the stitches are small.

When using a swing needle machine use a very small zig-zag stitch, about $\frac{1}{4}$ throw back. This will give more elasticity and at the same time be fine enough to enable the seam to be pressed flat. Some swing needle machines have special stitches for stretch and jersey fabrics.

Interfacings. Always use lightweight interfacing when it is necessary for parts of a garment to retain their shape or to be reinforced. Organdie, lawn or lightweight non-woven interlinings are suitable.

Underlining. Raschel knits should be underlined because of their openwork construction but it is not advisable to underline other types of jersey fabric unless this is done with another *knitted* fabric which will have the same elasticity. Woven fabrics will restrict the stretch of jersey fabrics. Bonded fabrics are, of course, already underlined.

Linings. Loose linings are often used for jersey fabrics and are attached to the garment just at the neck and along the edges of the zip fastener, sometimes at the armhole seams, and in skirts at the waist. Suitable fabric for lining is Tricel or lightweight taffeta.

Problems

1. Cotton and wool jerseys can shrink.
2. Fabrics are often knitted on circular machines so that they can be produced in tube form. The tube is then cut down one side and the opposite side is left folded. When the fabric is wound up on a bale this fold tends to become creased and is often difficult or almost impossible to press out.
3. As the fabrics stretch, the width can alter in handling. Single knits are stretchy and unstable and the weight of double knits can pull the fabric lengthwise and reduce the width.
4. Single knits, unless of the locknit variety, can ladder.
5. Thread used to stitch seams can break when strain is put upon it in wear.
6. Seam turnings roll and curl up.
7. Seams can stretch and drop after they have been stitched.

Dealing with the Problems

1. Roll the fabric up in a damp sheet overnight and press in the morning.
2. When planning the layout, fold the fabric so that the crease does not come on any part of the garment where it will show badly if it cannot be completely pressed out. Never arrange it to come down the centre front or back.
3. Always cut on a large flat surface so that the fabric can lie completely relaxed. If double knits and silk knits hang over the edge of a table, the weight of them may elongate the fabric and reduce the width. Any fabric which must lie off a table should be supported on a chair, or better still, it should be rolled up and rested on the end of the table. The pattern pieces can then be pinned onto the rest of the fabric, which can be rolled up with the pattern pieces as the layout proceeds.
4. Use fine hand and machine needles and preferably new ones. Check that the feed dog of the machine is not so sharp as to cause damage. A protective strip of tissue paper placed between it and the fabric will prevent damage and can be torn away after stitching. Remove tacking cotton carefully in quite short lengths to prevent it dragging the fabric and possibly damaging its structure. Try to avoid having to unpick any machine stitching as this can often cause laddering.
5. Use a small stitch or a zig-zag or a special stretch stitch when machining, and the correct type of thread.
6. Although knitted fabric does not fray, seam turnings should be neatened either by hand or by machine, as this will prevent them rolling under.
7. To avoid seams stretching, cut crossway strips of thin lining fabric 6 mm ($\frac{1}{4}$ in.) wide, or use purchased bias binding and cut it in half lengthwise to reduce the width. Place this strip centrally over the fitting line on one

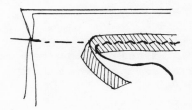

side of the seam and tack and stitch it in with the seam.

The stretch in the crossway strip will not restrict the elasticity of the jersey fabric more than is necessary to make it retain its original length. All seams should be treated in this way.

Curved edges of garments, such as necks, can be stay-stitched with a row of machining just outside the fitting line. This will help them to keep the correct shape and size.

Hang garments up overnight before levelling hems.

Processes

Seams. Plain seams should have the turnings neatened either by hand or by machine. When neatening by hand, blanket-stitch gives the best results.

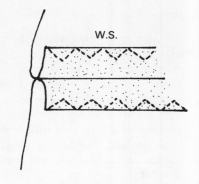

Seams for lingerie. These can be quite small because the fabric does not fray.
1. Tack and stitch the fitting lines together on the W.S.
2. Trim both turnings to 6 mm ($\frac{1}{4}$ in.) and neaten them together with machine zig-zag or by hand with blanket-stitch.

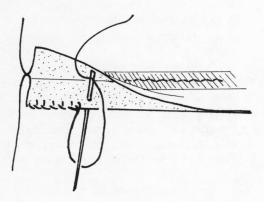

On a swing needle machine use the three-step zig-zag which is very elastic and will not tighten up the edge of the turnings.

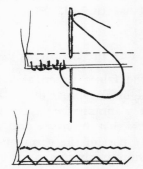

Top-stitched padded seams. These look very well on the heavier kinds of jersey. For a decorative effect buttonhole twist can be used in the machine, on the top only, although sometimes this can cause skipped stitches on jersey fabric. A better method is to use two reels of embroidery cotton size 30 on top, and thread them as one through the eye of the needle. Both methods produce a heavier, more noticeable stitching on the R.S. Lengthen the stitch to 8 per 2·5 cm (1 in.) or number 3 on a Continental machine.

1. On the W.S. tack and stitch the fitting lines together.
2. Trim down the inner turning so that it is just short of the top-stitching line. Trim the other turning

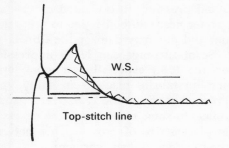

W.S.

Top-stitch line

so that it is 6 mm ($\frac{1}{4}$ in.) wider than the distance of the top-stitching from the seam.

3. Neaten the wider turning and fold it over the narrow one.
4. On the R.S., using a marker, make a

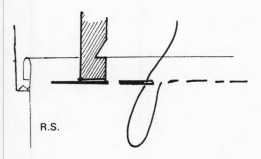

R.S.

line of straight tacking as a guide for the top-stitching. Machine along this line so that the narrow turning is enclosed by the stitching and forms a certain amount of padding.

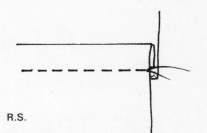

R.S.

Pockets. All pocket positions should be backed with interfacing to prevent stretching during wear.

Buttonholes. Interface to prevent stretching. All types of buttonhole are suitable, although machine-worked buttonholes are possibly the least suitable and are best worked over a cord.

Hems. As these fabrics tend to stretch more widthwise than lengthwise the stitches securing the hem should be kept fairly loose.

1. Neaten the raw edge of the hem with machine zig-zag or by hand with blanket stitch. If the hem is flared, lay buttonhole twist along the raw edge and work the neatening stitch over it. After neatening, pull up the twist and ease the flared hem edge along it to fit the garment.

21

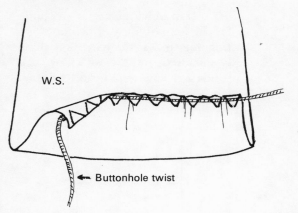

W.S.

← Buttonhole twist

2. Secure the hem in place with slip tacking, taking a good stitch into the hem turning and picking up only one thread from the garment. The stitches can be from 6 mm ($\frac{1}{4}$ in.) to 12 mm ($\frac{1}{2}$ in.) apart and the thread should be left as slack as is reasonable between them.

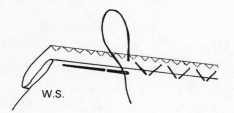

W.S.

Pressing

The temperature of the iron will depend on the fibre from which the fabric is made, i.e. fairly hot for cotton, warm for silk or wool and cool for rayons and synthetics and fabrics containing Lurex.

Synthetic fabrics, i.e. Courtelle, Crimplene, etc, should *not* be pressed damp nor with a damp cloth, because if they become stretched during pressing, damp heat can set the fabric in its stretched state. With these fabrics be careful to avoid pressing in unwanted creases as a greater heat will be needed to press them out and this may damage the fibres.

Seam turnings can leave impressions on the R.S., especially on wool jersey and on fabrics made from shiny yarn. Press all seams on the W.S. over a padded roller. In some cases it may be necessary to place strips of brown paper between the turnings and the garment.

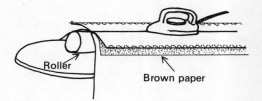

Roller

Brown paper

Cleaning

Wool and silk jersey fabrics should be dry-cleaned but those made from other fibres usually launder well. Synthetic fabrics can be drip-dried and should require very little if any ironing; however, where the weight of the water might cause them to stretch, they should be rinsed in *cold* water and then be given a quick spin – a few seconds only – in a spin drier, or they can be rolled in a towel and squeezed to press out the excess moisture. The cold water rinse is important because hot water can set creases in the fabric.

For special information on silk jersey, see chapter 1.

4. Towelling

Originally towelling was made for drying oneself but then people began to use it for bathroom curtains because of its moisture absorbency. When this happened manufacturers began to print interesting gay patterns on it whereas previously it had been mainly plain coloured or striped. From towels to curtains this fabric progressed to clothes for beach and day wear. At this stage stretch towelling was introduced as being more comfortable for clothes and babies' garments. There are therefore two main types of towelling:

Terry towelling. This can be loosely woven (cheaper types) or much more closely woven for better quality clothes and towels. One or both surfaces are covered with shaggy loops. The fabric has no elasticity.

Stretch towelling. This is a knitted fabric made from stretch yarn with a looped pile on one side only. It is comfortable to wear on account of its moisture absorbency and stretch.

The fibres used to make these fabrics can be cotton or linen for terry towelling, and cotton, with possibly a small percentage of synthetic fibre to set the stretch crimp in the yarn, for the stretch towelling.

Width. Terry towelling varies from 46 cm (18 in.) to 91 cm (36 in.). Stretch towelling varies from 91 cm (36 in.) to 172 cm (68 in.).

Uses. Terry towelling – Roller towels, bath towels and beach wear. Stretch towelling – Babies' wear, dresses, shorts and swim suits.

Styles. Almost any style except pleats, which might not press well.

Linings. Not often required as they would spoil the absorbent qualities of the fabric. If a lining is necessary use lawn or cambric.

Interfacings. If required use organdie as it is lightweight and retains its shape.

Sewing thread. Mercerised cotton size 40 for terry towelling. Synthetic thread for stretch towelling because it is more elastic.

Hand-sewing needles. Size 7 sharps.

Machine needle. Size 11 English or 70 Continental.

Machine stitch. 12 stitches per 2·5 cm (1 in.), dial 2 on Continental machines. For stretch towelling use the smallest zig-zag stitch, stitch length 2, stitch width $\frac{3}{4}$.

The problems of these two fabrics are different and will be dealt with separately.

Terry towelling problems

1. The fabric frays very badly, especially the loosely woven kind, and sheds 'crumbs' of thread.
2. When loosely woven the thread tends to pluck and catch in the feed of the machine and when pulled gathers the

fabric up along its entire width. It is almost impossible to work a pulled thread back again.

3. Unpicking machine stitching is not easy.

Dealing with the Problems (Terry towelling)

1. Leave wider turnings than usual when cutting out and avoid over handling the fabric.

2. Use a fine machine needle which will find its way between the threads. If the needle comes straight down on the thread it pulls it and distorts the fabric.

   Avoid catching the loops of the fabric on the machine feed by placing tissue paper between the fabric and the feed. This can be torn away after stitching.

3. Be accurate when tacking up and fit the garment carefully before machine stitching it.

Processes

Tailor tacking. This should be worked with tacking cotton of a contrasting colour, or it may become lost in the loops of the fabric.

Seams. Make the turnings deep enough so that the seams do not pull apart in wear.

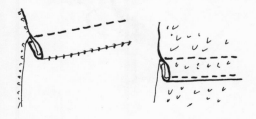

Welt and double stitched seams are quite the most satisfactory because they are strong and self-neatening.

If plain seams must be used the turnings should be neatened with crossway binding as overcasting would pull away on the loose weave.

Pockets. Lined patch pockets, pockets inset in a seam, and piped pockets made all in one piece, are the most satisfactory.

Fastenings. Worked buttonholes can be made if the fabric is backed with iron-on interfacing which will hold fraying threads together.

Piped buttonholes can be made as follows:

1. Mark the buttonhole positions with tacking.

2. Back the positions with iron-on interfacing.

3. Cut two straight grain strips of fabric 12 mm ($\frac{1}{2}$ in.) wide and 20 mm ($\frac{3}{4}$ in.) longer than each buttonhole and stick-iron on interfacing to the W.S.

4. Fold each strip exactly in half lengthwise and press well.

5. Place the strips either side of the buttonhole mark on the R.S. of the garment, with all the raw edges meeting over the buttonhole mark. See diagram.

6. Tack and machine for the exact length of the buttonhole *exactly* along the centre of each strip.

7. Cut the buttonhole in the fabric from the centre to within 6 mm ($\frac{1}{4}$ in.) of each end and then mitre right into each corner.

25

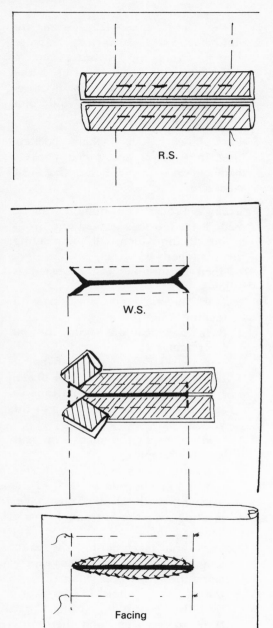

R.S.

W.S.

Facing

8. Push the strips through the slit to the W.S. so that their folded edges now meet in the centre.
9. Stitch the triangular sections at each end firmly to the piping.
10. Fold over the facing and tack in place all round the buttonhole about 12 mm ($\frac{1}{2}$ in.) away from the piping.
11. Cut a slit in the facing, turn the raw edges under with the point of a needle and hem firmly in place.

Corded frog fastenings are attractive and in keeping with the fabric.

If possible avoid using zip fasteners as the loops of the fabric could catch in the teeth of the zip and cause the slide to stick. Should it be necessary to use a zip, face the turnings of the seam with straight cut lawn before inserting the zip.

Hems. After levelling bind the raw edge with crossway strips of lawn or with purchased bias binding.

Slip hem into position or even use the blind hem on the sewing machine as any stitch which might show on the R.S. will be lost in the loopy pile of the fabric.

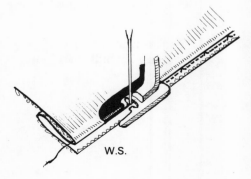

W.S.

Stretch towelling Problems

1. Some of these fabrics have a nap which causes shading if some parts of a garment are cut upside down.
2. The elasticity of the fabric can cause the seam stitching to split in wear.
3. Seam turnings tend to ripple when neatened by machine zig-zag.

Dealing with the Problems (Stretch towelling)

1. Check the fabric for nap by hanging it over a clothes line and comparing one half with the other. If it does differ in shade lay out the pattern pieces so that they all run in the direction in which the fabric looks darkest and richest.
2. If using a straight-stitch sewing machine the stitch must be small, 14 per 2·5 cm (1 in.), to prevent breakage.

   With a swing needle machine use a very small zig-zag stitch length 2, stitch width $\frac{3}{4}$.

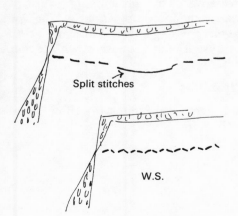

Split stitches

W.S.

On a fully automatic machine one of the special stretch stitches can be used.

Seams can be taped with bias-cut strips of lawn 6 mm ($\frac{1}{4}$ in.) wide, placed centrally over the fitting line and stitched in with the seam. The stretch in the bias will conform with the elasticity of the fabric.

3. See under Processes.

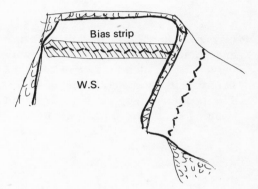

Bias strip

W.S.

Processes

Seams. Double-stitched, welt or plain seams can be used, bearing in mind that top-stitching restricts the stretch in the fabric.

When using zig-zag stitch to neaten the turnings of plain seams, stretching and rippling of the edge may take place. To prevent this, lay a fine cord, such as buttonhole twist, along the raw edge of the turning and work machine zig-zag stitch over the cord and the raw edge, being careful not to stitch through the cord. After stitching, the cord can be pulled up and the rippled edge of the turning eased along it until it is straight. See diagram overleaf.

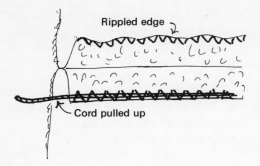

Rippled edge

Cord pulled up

Pockets. Patch pockets stretch with use and should be lined throughout with woven fabric such as lawn or cambric, before being attached to the garment. The pocket can be attached by hand seaming as shown in the diagram.

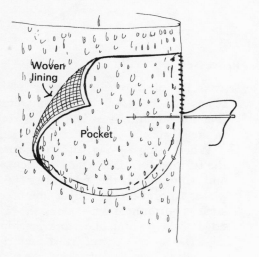

Woven lining

Pocket

Welt pockets should be interlined with iron-on interlining, to prevent stretching.

Fastenings. Piped buttonholes can be made as described for terry towelling.

Worked buttonhole positions must be backed with organdie and can be worked by hand or machine over fine cord which will help to prevent stretching. Large press studs can be used.

Curved edges. Make a row of machine stitching on the turnings close to the fitting line as a stay against stretching.

When attaching a facing to a curved edge a narrow 6 mm ($\frac{1}{4}$ in.) strip of straight cut organdie should be stitched in with the seam.

Hems. After levelling bind the edge with crossway lawn or zig-zag the edge by machine over buttonhole twist which can be pulled up to make the edge of the hem fit the garment. Tack the hem in place and slip the hem by hand or use the blind-hem on the sewing machine.

Pressing. This presents no difficulty. Use a medium hot iron on the W.S. Avoid pressing stretch fabric on the R.S., because it might squash down the loops.

Cleaning

Both terry and stretch towelling launder well.

These include fabrics such as Lycra, stretch jerseys, stretch towelling and stretch linens and denims. They are fabrics either woven or knitted from yarn which stretches. The yarn may be 1) a rubber core with an outer covering or 2) it may be made from thermoplastic fibre which can be moulded with moisture and heat and set permanently into a tight crimp which will spring back when released after being stretched.

Woven fabrics may stretch across the width (weft stretch), down the length (warp stretch), or both across and down (weft and warp stretch) – a type used mainly for swim suits.

Knitted fabrics stretch both ways but usually rather more across the fabric than lengthwise.

Uses. The stretch enables garments to fit tightly while at the same time being comfortable to wear, e.g. trousers, swim suits, corsetry. The stretch prevents skirts from 'seating'.

Styles. These fabrics can be made up into almost any style suitable for the weight and type being used.

Sewing threads. Synthetic threads and pure sewing silk are the best to use because they are elastic and will stretch with the fabric.

Machine needle. Size 11 or 14 English, 70 or 80 Continental, depending on the weight of the fabric.

Hand-sewing needle. Size 8 or 7.

Machine stitch. Small stitches are less likely to break with strain. 15 stitches per 2·5 cm (1 in.) or setting 1 or 1½ on a Continental sewing machine.

Interfacing. Non-woven, organdie and lightweight canvas are suitable.

Problems

1. The stretch properties of the fabrics must not be put out of action when making up.
2. Sewing thread is not so elastic as the fabric and could snap when stretched in wear.
3. A hot iron can upset the stretch.

Ways of dealing with the Problems

1. a. Do not underline. b. Unless you want to prevent them stretching, do not tape seams. c. Do not use seam binding on hems. d. When using a loose lining, make it from a knitted fabric which will 'give' with stretch. e. Do not press the fabric under a damp cloth when it is stretched as this could set it permanently in its stretched state.
2. Many sewing machines have special stretch stitches for these fabrics and they are ideal. When using swing needle machines which do not have

these stitches use a very small zig-zag stitch length $1\frac{1}{2}$, stitch width just off the straight stitch mark. Do not stretch the fabric when stitching.

When using a straight stitch machine, set it for a short stitch.

Processes

Preparation of fabric. It is advisable to shrink the fabric before cutting out. For this use a steam iron and just press by lifting the iron up and down all over the fabric and then pat the steam away. Do not, on any account, push the iron across the fabric as this may stretch it.

Layout. Arrange all pattern pieces so that the stretch is running in the required direction, i.e. across the pattern for dresses, skirts and blouses and down the length for slacks with foot straps. Often the fabric can be turned round to get the stretch in the required direction.

Be careful not to stretch the fabric when pinning the pattern to it. Lay everything flat on the table so that the fabric is quite relaxed.

Seams. Use plain seams neatened with overcasting or zig-zag machine stitching.

Top-stitched seams are possible but not ideal as a small machine stitch has to be used to keep the stretch in the fabric and for this purpose it does not look particularly attractive.

On stretch towelling and other knitted fabrics the following seam can be used; stitch the fitting lines together on the W.S., then trim the turnings to 6 mm ($\frac{1}{4}$ in.) and machine zig-zag them together.

Pockets. Patch pockets are suitable but they should be lined with a woven lining fabric to prevent stretching and sagging in wear.

Welt pockets should be interlined with non-stretch woven fabric. Piped and bound pockets should be backed with woven interfacing cut on the straight grain.

Fastenings. Any type of fastening is suitable. Buttonhole positions should be interfaced with woven fabric cut on the straight grain.

Worked buttonholes should be stranded whether worked by hand or machine, otherwise they may stretch and the botton will slip out (see diagram opposite).

Hems. Do not ever use seam binding on a hem as this will stop the fabric stretching. The raw edge of a hem should be neatened either with machine zig-zag or by turning the edge under and edge-stitching it (see diagram).

The hem is then slip-stitched into position; be careful not to pull the thread too tight.

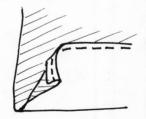

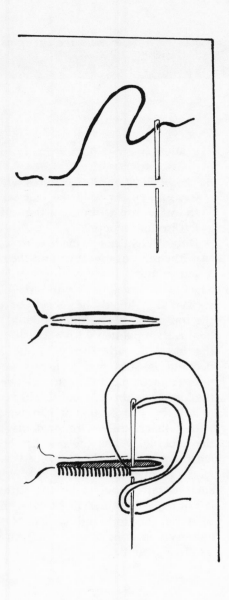

Pressing

Press under dry muslin with a warm iron, never a hot one. Press seams over a roller to avoid an imprint on the R.S. Always press the iron up and down and do not glide it over the fabric as this could stretch it.

Cleaning and care

Fabrics made from yarn containing a rubber core should be hand-washed in warm soapy water. Do not use chemical detergents as these have a damaging effect on the rubber. Let them drip-dry and only touch up with an iron if necessary.

Fabrics made from other types of stretch yarn may be dry-cleaned or washed with soap or detergent, by hand or in a washing machine and then allowed to drip-dry. Always pay attention to any cleaning or washing instructions given with the fabric when it is purchased and, if this is in the form of a 'sew in' label be sure to sew it into the garment for future reference. If, after wearing them for a time, skirts and slacks appear to have seated a little, hang them up to allow the fabric to relax into its original shape. Very occasionally it will be necessary to press the garment back into shape.

6. Velvet

This is a fabric with a short dense pile woven into a backing which has either a plain or twill weave or is knitted. The pile may be smoothed down flat in one direction or it may be smoothed partly in one direction and partly in the opposite way, or it may stand erect like a brush. Originally velvet was made from silk and velveteen from cotton, but not now. Often it is made with a cotton or linen backing and the pile may be made from silk, cotton or rayon, and sometimes both the backing and the pile are made entirely from synthetic fibres such as nylon. The pile can vary in depth from 2 mm ($\frac{1}{16}$ in.) to 3 mm ($\frac{1}{8}$ in.).

The fabric is made by various methods such as the following:

1. Two backing fabrics are woven, slightly apart facing each other, while the pile is woven in between them from one to the other. The pile is then cut down the centre between the backings, separating them into two lengths of velvet fabric.

2. a. The pile is woven into a single backing by being looped over wires which have a knife edge. After it has been woven over four of these wires the first one is withdrawn and the knife cuts through the loops leaving a pile of tufts. Then the weaving continues over the next wire and the second wire is withdrawn, making another pile of tufts and so on.

   b. The pile is looped over wires which have no cutting edge so that when the wires are withdrawn the pile is left in uncut loops.

   Note: Velvet can be made with some of the pile cut into tufts and the rest left in uncut loops.

3. The pile is woven loosely into the base so that the threads lie loosely across the top surface. The underside of the base is then painted with paste to hold the loose threads firmly, while the backing is stretched tightly, and a pointed instrument is pushed between the loose pile threads and the backing to lift the pile so that it can be cut with a sharp knife without damaging the backing. When the pile has been cut the paste is washed away.

4. Flock printed velvet has a backing such as taffeta on which the pattern is printed with adhesive. Flock is then scattered on top and sticks to the adhesive, forming a raised pattern on a taffeta ground.

TYPES OF VELVET

Chiffon velvet. A very fine lightweight velvet which has the pile pressed flat in one direction.

Ciselé velvet. A type of embossed velvet with part of the pile cut and part left in loops.

Costume velvet. Velvet with a cotton or rayon pile on a strong cotton backing.

Cotton velvets. a. Velveteen, nowadays called cotton velvet, is a plain or printed velvet with both pile and backing made from cotton.

b. Corduroy is a strong fabric with a cotton base. The pile may be cotton or rayon and is made by weft threads being looped up with extra weft threads, worked in to form a ribbed surface. The ribs may vary in width.

c. Needlecord and corded velvet are similar in appearance to corduroy but have very fine ribs. They may be plain or have a pattern printed on them.

Crushed velvet. Has been treated to make it look as though it had been crumpled up. Areas of the pile are flattened in one direction and other areas in the opposite direction so that it looks light in some places and dark in others, giving a crushed effect.

Cut velvet. This is chiffon or voile fabric with a brocade type of pattern woven into it in a velvet pile.

Façonné velvet. Resembles cut velvet in appearance. It is woven as plain velvet and then the unwanted background of the design is printed with a chemical which burns it out leaving the pattern standing as a velvet relief on a sheer ground.

Nacré velvet. The pile is woven in a different colour from the backing.

Lyons velvet. This is used mainly for hats. It has a short erect pile and the backing can be seen quite clearly through it.

Panne velvet. Has the pile pressed flat in one direction which gives it a shimmering appearance.

Lurex velvet. The pile is made partly from Lurex thread which adds sparkle to the fabric.

Uses

Velvets are no longer confined to evening wear and day-time trimmings. Modern velvets do not fingerprint like those of former days and can now be used for daytime wear such as tunics, slacks, dresses and coats provided the right type of velvet is used for each garment. For example, crushed velvet can be used for slacks, panne velvets for tunics and dresses and the more expensive sculptured, cut and Lurex velvets for evening coats, capes and wraps, and the stronger cotton velvets and corduroys for day-time coats.

Styles

Choose styles with simple lines and few seams which will not detract from the beauty of the fabric. It will be the fabric which will make the dress rather than the style interest. At all costs avoid any top-stitching which will either sink into the pile or spoil it. Pleats are definitely out, because the fabric cannot be pressed to form pleats. It is possible to introduce a limited amount of gathering and parts can be cut on the cross but this may cause a shaded effect because the pile is cut in a different direction from other parts of the garment cut on the straight grain.

Choose styles with button loops rather than buttonholes which do not look at all good on this fabric.

Remember to buy the amount of fabric stated on the pattern envelope for fabrics *with nap* because all the pattern pieces have to be laid in the same direction when cutting out and cannot be turned upside down to fit in more economically. This means that some of the fabric must be cut to waste and it may be necessary to buy extra.

Width. 0·91 m (36 in.).

Sewing thread. For silk velvets use pure sewing silk.

For cotton velvets use mercerised cotton size 40.

For synthetic velvets use synthetic threads.

For tacking use pure sewing silk as this marks the fabric less than tacking cotton.

Hand-sewing needles. Size 7 or 8 sharps.

Machine needle. Use fine needles size 11 English, 70 Continental.

Machine stitch. Use a long stitch to avoid puckering the material. 8 stitches per 2·5 cm (1 in.) or setting 3 on a Continental machine.

Problems

1. The fabric has a pile, usually running in one direction.
2. Pins and tacking can leave marks which are difficult to remove. Alterations usually show.
3. The fabric walks along on itself because of the pile.
4. Seams have a tendency to quilt or pucker, when stitched.
5. Some fabrics can fingermark badly.
6. Pressing can flatten the pile.

Dealing with the Problems

1. The pile in cotton velvet, corduroy and needlecord should smooth downwards on a garment. The pile on other velvets usually smooths upwards.

   The general rule is that the right way up is the way that the fabric looks darkest. When in doubt (this can happen when the pile is erect) hang the fabric up, first one way and then the other way and look at it from a distance to find out which way it looks darkest and richest. The best way to do this is to loop it twice over a rail so that the two directions of the pile will be side by side and the difference can then be seen more easily.

   The layout may be extravagant as all pattern pieces must be placed so that the pile runs in the same direction.

2. Use fine needles instead of pins to hold parts together. When fixing the paper pattern in position, put the needles into the turning allowance where any marks they may make will not show when the garment is made up. For tacking use fine sewing silk which is less likely to mark the fabric. The fitting lines should be traced out accurately with flat tacking in place of tailor tacking. This will make assembling more accurate and the

fabric is less likely to be damaged when the tacking is removed. Be very accurate with the fitting and stitch carefully to avoid having to make any alterations.

3. After fitting replace the needles at intervals across the seam turnings and take the machine needle carefully over them when stitching. This should prevent the movement of the fabric on itself.

4. Place tissue paper between the sections to be joined and stitch through all thicknesses. The paper can be torn away afterwards and this will loosen the tension slightly and help to release the tightness caused by the thickness of the pile. It helps also if the fabric is held taut during stitching and if the pressure of the presser foot is reduced a little.

5. Fingermarks can usually be removed by holding the fabric for a few moments in the steam from a boiling kettle.

6. Needlecord and corduroy may be pressed on the W.S. under a damp cloth in the usual way without damaging the pile. Other velvets need extreme care. Adjust the iron temperature to suit the fibre from which the fabric is made. If one is available, use a needleboard and then pressing will be no problem. Without a needleboard seams may be pressed face down over another piece of velvet. Alternatively, the fabric can be held up by two people and stretched taut and then the iron can be passed over the seams on the W.S. Yet another way is to stand the iron up on end, place a damp cloth over it and then run the W.S. of a seam back and forth over it. To avoid impressions of turnings showing on the R.S. place strips of strong brown paper between the turnings and the garment before pressing.

Processes

Cutting out. It is much safer to cut out each piece singly. Lay the fabric face downwards and arrange the pattern pieces on the W.S. When only half the pattern is supplied chalk round it and then reverse it to cut the other side. To ensure that the pattern is so placed that the pile runs the right way mark the direction of the pile on the W.S. with small chalked arrows.

Seams. Use plain seams and neaten them by hand overcasting, or by machine zig-zag (stitch width 3, stitch length $1\frac{1}{2}$) or with a narrow binding of jap silk.

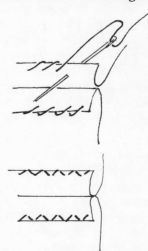

35

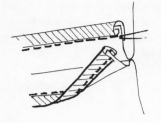

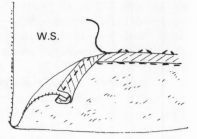

Pockets. For dresses, those inserted in a seam are best. On velvet jackets welt and patch pockets can be used. Patch pockets should be lined with jap silk and then applied to the garment by hand, thus avoiding top-stitching.

Fastenings. Buttons and worked loops are suitable for velvet and piped buttonholes can be used for corduroy and needlecord. Piped buttonholes are not very good for velvet as with use the pile becomes flattened and looks shabby. Worked buttonholes, using buttonhole twist, can be made successfully. Frog fastenings look good on these fabrics. Zip fasteners can be used and are best put in entirely by hand, unless they are of the invisible type when they can be machined in from the W.S. Eyelet holes with lacing and Velcro burr fastenings are also possible.

Hems. Level the hem, fold it to the inside, holding it in place with fine needles. Trim it to the required depth and neaten the raw edge with hand overcasting, machine zig-zag or with a jap silk binding as shown in the diagram. The hem turning will now have to be carefully tacked and slip-hemmed into place. Remove the tacking in short lengths without dragging the pile off the fabric.

When the hem is flared the raw edge should be overcast or zig-zagged over buttonhole twist without catching the twist in the stitching. The twist can then be pulled up to ease the surplus fabric of the hem to fit the garment, before slip-stitching. When the hem is very flared or circular, the garment should be hung up for a day or so before the hem is levelled to allow the weight of the fabric to drop. The hem turning should then be levelled off to 6 mm ($\frac{1}{4}$ in.) below the level line and the raw edge can be finished with a narrow facing of jap silk on the W.S.

Velvet hems should not be pressed or the pile will be flattened.

Care of velvet

Some velvets are washable nowadays, but others have to be dry-cleaned. Always ask which kind they are when buying them. Needlecord and corduroy can be washed and hung up to drip-dry to avoid creasing. Tack a label inside a velvet garment stating the fibre from which the fabric is made. This is important when it has to be pressed so that the correct temperature may be used, and when it has to be dry-cleaned it may prevent harmful cleaning agents being used which might damage the fabric.

7. Fur fabrics

Fur fabrics can be made to imitate real furs very closely; they can have a short or long pile and be shaggy, smooth or textured. They are usually made from synthetic fibres such as nylon worked into a knitted backing.

Width. 1·32 m (52 in.) wide.

Properties. Fur fabrics are warm to wear. The fibres trap air between them which insulates against cold.

They are comfortable to wear – more so than real fur – because there is more 'give' in the knitted backing fabric and they are much lighter in weight.

The fabrics are hygienic because many of them can be washed.

Uses. Adults' and children's coats, hoods and hats. Trimmings for coats and dresses.

Styles. Choose simple styles with few seams and not too fitted. Avoid top-stitched styles because the stitching would sink into the pile.

Sewing threads. Synthetic threads and mercerised cotton size 40.

Hand-sewing needle. Size 7 sharps.

Machine needle. Size 14.

Machine stitch. Use a rather long stitch as the fabric is bulky and might pucker. 8 stitches per 2·5 cm (1 in.), and on Continental machines turn the dial to $2\frac{1}{2}$–3.

Interfacings. Non-woven interfacings, organdie, fine hair canvas.

Linings. Taffeta, Tricel.

Problems

1. Fur fabric has a pile generally smoothing in one direction.
2. It cannot be cut double like most fabrics.
3. Tailor tacking is not satisfactory because the threads can be lost in the pile and are difficult to remove.
4. Pile can get caught in the seam when it is stitched.
5. It cannot be stitched from the R.S. because the pile catches in the feed-dog.
6. Buttonholes are not possible.

Ways of dealing with the Problems

1. Check the direction of the pile and arrange pattern pieces so that it will smooth downwards from collar to hem. As pattern pieces must be laid on the W.S. singly, mark the direction of the pile on the back of the fabric with chalked arrows (see diagram).
2. Pin the pattern to the back of the fabric and cut the pieces out with a sharp razor blade, cutting through the backing fabric only and not through the pile. Pull the pile apart so that in this way it remains intact and is not cut.
3. Fold the turning allowance on the pattern back to the fitting line, clipping across curved turnings to make

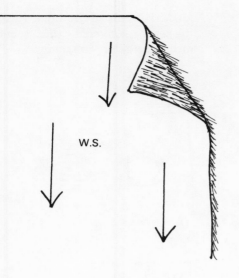

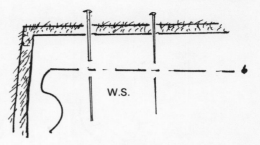

them lie flat. Chalk the fitting lines on the fabric. Use dressmakers' carbon paper to mark the dart positions.

4. After stitching a seam turn the work over to the R.S. and with a needle lever out any of the pile that has been caught into the stitching and brush it gently in the direction of the pile, smoothing it over the join to conceal it.

5. Top-stitching should not be necessary if the correct style for the fabric has been chosen.

6. Use elastic loops for buttonholes. Large covered hooks and eyes are suitable, and possibly frogs made from cord.

Processes

Seams. a. Pin fitting lines together with the pins placed *across* the seam turnings to prevent the top layer moving along on the pile of the lower one.

Tack with smallish stitches. Remove the pins when fitting and replace them when stitching up the seam, taking the machine needle carefully over each one as it is encountered.

Make plain seams and press open with the toe of the iron.

Turn the work over to the R.S. and flick out any of the pile that has been trapped in the stitching.

b. Some fur fabrics are striped and where the stripes have to be matched, in order to avoid waste, take up the smallest possible turnings 3 mm ($\frac{1}{8}$ in.) when joining sections. After stitching, overcast or machine zig-zag the turnings together.

Darts. After stitching, split open and press flat and then flick out any pile caught in on the R.S.

Pockets. In some instances patch pockets could be used. Line them with lining material and then seam them on to the garment by hand.

Pockets made from lining material and inset in a seam are the most suitable.

Fastenings.

1. Fur coat elastic loops. The elastic is a thick type made specially for the

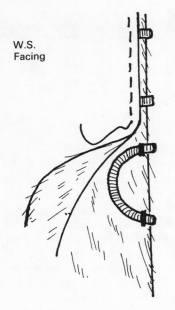

W.S.
Facing

R.S.

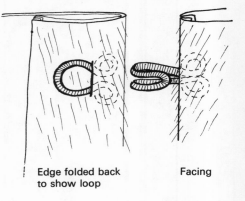

Edge folded back
to show loop

Facing

push the ends of the hook through the seam and oversew them securely to the inside of the facing.

Note. If the facing is cut all in one with the front and folded back, a small slit must be made in the fold and the hook pushed through so that it can be stitched on the inside. Find the position for the eye and here make the smallest possible slit. Push the ends of the eye through it and stitch them to the back of the fabric.

3. Twist cord into frogs and stitch in place, then stab stitch them strongly to the garment. Button moulds can be covered quite successfully with some fur fabrics.

Hems. If the chalk of a hem marker will not show up on a fur fabric the level line will have to be marked with pins, preferably pins with coloured heads which will be conspicuous, because

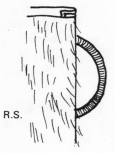

purpose. Insert them in the seam of the facing as for rouleau loops (see diagram).

2. Large hooks and eyes are made specially for furs. Use a matching colour and sew on as follows: When a separate facing is stitched to the front of a coat, unpick a few stitches where the hook is to be put on,

ordinary pins can get buried in the pile of the fabric and be overlooked.

Turn the hem up and catch-stitch or slip-hem it to the knitted backing; the stitches are very unlikely to show through on the R.S. of the garment.

The hem of the lining of a coat is best left loose and just caught to the coat seams with French tacks.

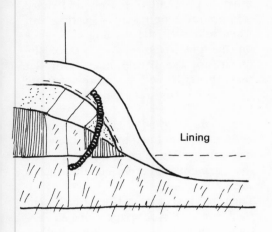

Lining

Pressing

Always use a cool iron because the fabric can be damaged by too much heat. Press seams open on the W.S. under dry muslin, using only the toe of the iron to run along the join, in order not to flatten down the pile on the R.S. of the fabric.

The lining is most easily pressed if it is left loose at the hem because the ironing board can be slipped between the lining and the fabric.

Care of fur fabric

Some fur fabrics can be washed gently and drip-dried. On the whole they are better dry-cleaned.

When not in use store them in a plastic bag because these synthetic fibres collect a certain amount of static electricity and this attracts dust which could make light-coloured and white fur fabrics look grubby.

8. Quilted fabrics

Fabrics can be bought already quilted. Some fabrics are lined and some not. The outer covering is usually cotton or nylon and the inner padding is Courtelle or Tricel wadding, all of which are washable.

Uses. Dressing gowns, bed jackets, anoraks, linings and sleeping bags.

Width. 0·91 m (36 in.).

Styles. Choose plain styles with few seams. The fabric, although lightweight, is bulky and hangs stiffly so that any drapery is out of the question.

Thread. Use mercerised cotton size 50 or synthetic threads.

Machine needle. Size 11 English or 70 Continental.

Size of machine stitch. 8 stitches per 2·5 cm (1 in.), stitch length 3 on Continental machines.

Hand-sewing needle. Sharps size 8.

Problems

1. The fabric is thick and tailor tacking is not easy, also it sticks in the wadding and is difficult to remove.
2. When the fabric is lined the seams will show on the inside and will require neatening.
3. Seams tend to pucker.
4. Facings can be bulky.
5. When the fabric is unlined the wadding side is inclined to catch and tear on the feed dog of the machine.

Ways of dealing with the Problems

1. The fabric is bouncy so the pattern must be pinned on securely and sharp scissors must be used for cutting out. Then fold back the turning allowance on the pattern pieces and trace the outline of the fitting lines with flat tacking. This will be more accurate and easier to remove than tailor tacking.
2. When making a dressing gown or bedjacket from lined material the seam neatening must be good because when the garment is taken off the inside shows.
3. The thickness of the fabric causes seam puckering. Tissue paper placed between the two layers of fabric before stitching and torn away afterwards will produce a slightly looser stitch which will help to prevent puckering. Use a long machine stitch.
4. If a centre front facing can be cut in one with the front and folded back instead of a separate facing being stitched on, the folded edge will be less bulky than a stitched seam.
5. Place tissue paper between the feed-dog of the machine and the wadding side of unlined fabric to prevent the wadding being torn. Tear the paper away afterwards.

Processes

Seams. When the fabric is unlined use a plain seam pressed open. It will not show because the lining will cover it when it is put in.

When the fabric is already lined more attention must be paid to the seams as they must be very neat.

1. Stitch the seam along the fitting lines on the W.S. and trim to 6 mm ($\frac{1}{4}$ in.) and blanket stitch or machine zig-zag the turnings together.
2. Stitch a plain seam, press it open and trim the turnings to 12 mm ($\frac{1}{2}$ in.) and then bind the raw edges as follows:
   a. Cut crossway strips of a thin matching fabric 18 mm ($\frac{3}{4}$ in.) wide.
   b. Stitch the strip to the R.S. of the turning a quarter of its depth in from the raw edges.
   c. Fold the crossway strip over the raw edges to the W.S. and from the R.S. stitch through the turning to hold the underside of the binding in place (see diagram).

3. A neat method would be a machine and fell seam worked as follows:
   a. Stitch a plain seam.
   b. Trim the front turning to 6 mm ($\frac{1}{4}$ in.) and the back turning to 12 mm ($\frac{1}{2}$ in.). Press the wider turning over the smaller one.
   c. On the inside of the wider turning cut away the wadding and the inner layer of covering material, leaving just lining material. Fold the raw edge of the lining material under for 6 mm ($\frac{1}{4}$ in.) and hem the folded edge to the garment.

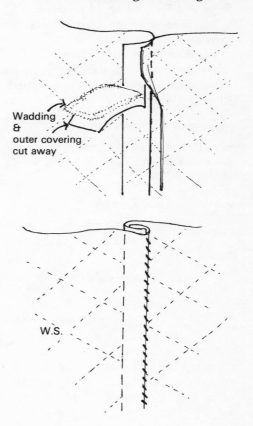

Wadding & outer covering cut away

W.S.

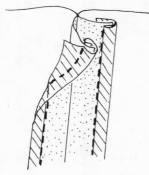

Darts. Cut down the fold and press open as the fabric is too bulky to leave the dart folded. When using lined fabric finish by one of the methods suggested for a seam.

Pockets. Patch pockets are the most suitable. When using unlined fabric the pocket should be lined before attaching it to the garment because the wadding would not be durable enough if not covered.

Pockets could be inset in a seam.

Fastenings. For dressing gowns, corded frogs and buttons could be used.

Machine-worked buttonholes are possible.

Worked loops and buttons.

For anoraks and sleeping bags use zip-fasteners, open-ended type, stitched on by machine.

Interfacings. These are not required.

Hems. Either overcast, machine zig-zag or bind the raw edge as described for binding a seam. After neatening slipstitch the hem in position. These methods apply to self-lined fabric. When the fabric is not lined the hem will be covered by the lining of the garment.

Pressing

Press very lightly, using only the toe of the iron to open seams out. Heavy pressing will squash down the puffiness of the quilting. The temperature of the iron will depend on the fibre from which the covering fabric is made, i.e. cool for nylon and hotter for cotton, bearing in mind that the wadding is synthetic and could be damaged by too much heat.

Cleaning

Everything is washable. For best results drip-dry and shake the garment occasionally to fluff out the wadding. If necessary touch up as lightly as possible with the iron.

These fabrics consist of the following types:

1. Fabric fused to foam.
2. Two layers of fabric with foam sandwiched between them. This is known as coin-bonded fabric.
3. Two woven fabrics bonded together as in double-faced coatings.
4. Woven fabric bonded to a knitted backing fabric.
5. Two knitted fabrics bonded to each other, back to back. These have more stretch than woven fabrics bonded to knitted backings.
6. Lace bonded to a backing fabric or to net.

The advantages of these fabrics are that they do not fray, do not usually need underlining, which cuts down work and expense, and they are very lightweight and warm to wear.

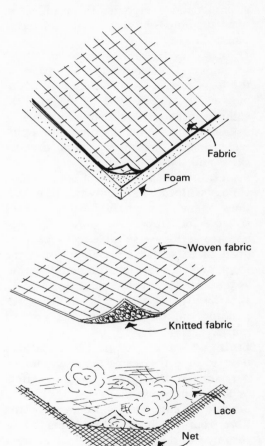

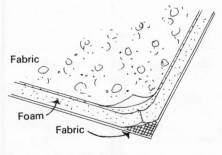

Coin-bonded

The layers of fabric can be attached to each other with adhesive or by using thermoplastic fibres which melt with heat and moisture and fuse the fabrics together.

The fused underlining gives body to the outer fabric and is particularly useful in helping a loosely woven stretchy fabric to keep its shape. A coloured underlining bonded to lace will give decorative interest as well as added strength and overcomes the problem of seam turnings showing through a transparent fabric.

Uses. Types 1, 2 and 3 are used mainly for anoraks and coats. The air spaces in the foam provide a considerable amount of warmth and, weight for weight, are claimed to be warmer than single fabric.

Types 4, 5 and 6 are used for lightweight coats, dressmaker suits, dresses, skirts and slacks.

Styles. Except in the case of bonded lace, choose sculptured styles with rather stiff lines as most of these fabrics are not suitable for drapery or gathering. Topstitched styles are suitable and look very good in these fabrics. When using the foam-backed types choose simple styles as these are less easy to make up.

Interfacings. Use organdie or Vilene depending on the weight of the bonded fabric.

Linings. Loose linings are sometimes used to hide the seams inside garments. Any suitable lining fabric such as taffeta or Tricel can be used.

Sewing thread. This will depend on the fibre from which the fabric is made. For cottons and rayons use mercerised cotton size 40.

For synthetic fabrics use synthetic thread.

Hand-sewing needle. Size 7 sharps, though this depends rather on the thickness of the fabric.

Machine needle. Size 11 English or 70 Continental for foam-backed fabric and for kits.

Size 14 English, 80 Continental for double faced woollens.

Machine stitch. For bonded lace 14 stitches per 2·5 cm (1 in.) or 1½ on Continental machines. For medium weight fabrics 12 stitches per 2·5 cm (1 in.) or dial 2 and for heavy fabrics 10 stitches per 2·5 cm (1 in.) or dial 2½ on Continental machines.

Problems

1. The top side of the fabric is sometimes badly bonded so that it is off grain. This is particularly noticeable when the fabric is patterned or knitted, and the ribs of the knitting are not running straight.
2. Foam-backed fabric sticks on the feed of the machine and will not glide through.
3. A hot iron can damage the foam.
4. When the fabric is thick the seams are somewhat bulky and will not press very flat.

Dealing with the Problems

1. Examine the roll of fabric carefully before purchasing to make sure that the fabric has been bonded with the grain running straight.
2. Spray the plate, feed and needle of the sewing machine with silicone spray.

   Place tissue paper between the foam and the feed dog when stitching and tear this away afterwards. Alternatively, tape the seams, placing the tape between the feed dog and the foam. Sprinkle talcum powder or French chalk over the foam before stitching.

With coin-bonded fabric the difficulty does not arise because the foam is enclosed.

Use a fine machine needle so that it can be withdrawn easily from the foam.

3. Use a moderate iron when pressing and always use a pressing cloth between the iron and the foam, or press the garment on the R.S.
4. Thin out seams on foam-backed fabric by cutting them down to 6 mm ($\frac{1}{4}$ in.); they will not fray, so this is possible. Cut darts open and trim them down to 6 mm ($1\frac{1}{4}$ in.) also.

Another method is to pare the foam down on the turnings. With special adhesive, such as upholstery solution, seam turnings can be stuck down, but be careful about the kind of adhesive as some types shrivel the foam up and make it hard.

Processes

Preparation of material is not necessary beyond checking the straightness of the grain.

Cutting out. When the fabric is foam-backed cut out each pattern piece singly because it is difficult to cut accurately through double bulky material.

Tailor tackings will stick in the foam and be difficult to remove, so mark the fitting lines on the foam side with chalk.

Seams. Plain and top-stitched seams look good on the bulky types of fabric. Use plain seams on lacy types.

Although these fabrics do not fray, the seam turnings look better neatened if the garment is not lined. They can be overcast or machine zig-zagged. For unlined coats neaten the turnings with crossway binding cut from thin lining fabrics.

Neck and armhole facings cut from lining will reduce bulk.

Sleeves. When using foam-backed or coin-bonded fabrics choose raglan styles which are easier to manage than set-in sleeves where it would be difficult to disperse the surplus material at the head of the sleeve.

Fastenings. Almost any type of fastening can be used.

Pressing

The temperature of the iron will depend on the fibre from which the fabric is made. If, for instance, cotton is bonded to a synthetic backing the iron must be cool and set for the weaker material, i.e. the nylon. It is always best to press under a cloth.

Owing to the bulky nature of the fabrics imprints of seam turnings may occur on the R.S. and when this happens press the seams over a roller. Never let the iron touch the foam of a foam-backed fabric.

Cleaning

Wash or dry-clean according to the fibre from which the fabric is made. Most bonded fabrics wash well.

Foam-backed fabric will wash easily in hot but not boiling water. Make sure that both the foam and the fabric are quite dry before pressing. These fabrics will also dry-clean.

10. Double-faced reversible fabrics

This is made up of two separate fabrics back to back. Usually one fabric is checked or patterned and the other is often plain but can be patterned also. The two layers of fabric are either stitched together loosely inside, or are bonded or fused together with adhesive. The first method is possibly a little easier to handle than the other. Both layers of fabric are usually made from wool.

Uses. Reversible top coats

Width. 138 cm (54 in.).

Styles. Choose simple, loose styles with as few seams as possible. Raglan and kimono-type sleeves are easier to cope with than set-in sleeves as the fullness round the head is difficult to dispose of in the latter type. Single- and double-breasted coats are suitable and only patch pockets can be made.

Sewing threads. Pure sewing silk or mercerised cotton size 40.

Hand-sewing needles. Sharps size 8.

Machine needle. Size 14 English or 80 Continental.

Machine stitch. 10–12 per 2·5 cm (1 in.) or dial $2\frac{1}{2}$–2 on Continental sewing machines.

Interfacings. Not possible.

Linings. Not required.

Problems

1. Seams and darts must look alike on both sides.

2. Buttons and buttonholes must be reversible.

3. Hems and facings are not possible.

Dealing with the Problems

1. Use plain or welt seams worked as shown under processes.

2. Arrange buttons and buttonholes as shown under processes.

3. Edges can be bound with braid or turned in on themselves and slip-stitched.

Special note. Sometimes the fabric on one side is a completely different colour from the fabric on the other side and when this happens two different matching sewing threads will have to be used, one on the bobbin of the sewing machine and the other on top. Do not forget to keep the right side uppermost when machining.

Processes

Seams – Plain seam.

1. Separate the two layers of fabric along the turnings as far as 12 mm ($\frac{1}{2}$ in.) inside the fitting lines, by snipping the loose stitches between, which hold them together. Note that it is possible to work a plain seam only on fabric that is stitched

together, as the bonded type cannot be pulled apart.

2. Place the plain side of one section to the plain side of the other and tack up and stitch the turnings on the fitting line of the plain fabric only. Press the seam open.

3. On the patterned side fold the turnings under to the fitting line so that the folded edges just meet over the stitched seam and then all the turnings will be inside. Tack the top turnings in place and slip-stitch the folded edges together.

It is better to stitch the plain side first because any checks and stripes on the patterned side can be more easily matched with hand sewing.

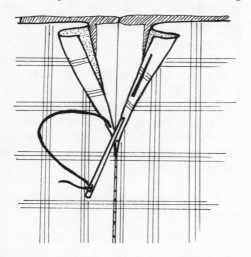

Welt seams. These can be worked on either type of double fabric.

Method 1

a. Place the two pieces of fabric together and tack and stitch on the fitting line.

b. Cut down one of the turnings to 3 mm ($\frac{1}{8}$ in.) and the other to 15 mm ($\frac{5}{8}$ in.).

c. Press the wider turning over the narrow one, turn the raw edge under and tack and machine in place.

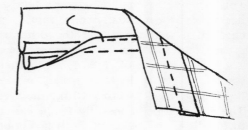

Method 2

a. Lap one raw edge over the other until the fitting lines of each section lie exactly on top of each other. Pin together through the fitting lines.

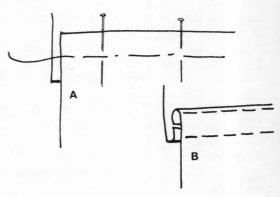

b. Trim each turning to 12 mm ($\frac{1}{2}$ in.) and fold the edges under until they meet the fitting line.

c. Tack and machine along the folded edges as in the diagram.

This method is the better one to use when the coat is intended to be truly reversible, as both sides look exactly alike.

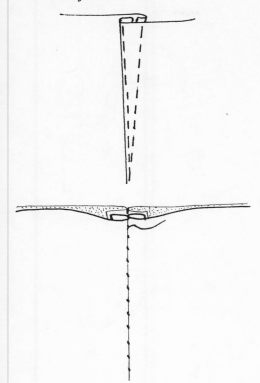

Darts. Stitch darts, using the method described for a plain seam. When the fabrics are bonded the dart must be stitched as for a welt seam, method 2.

Pockets.

1. Cut out the pockets and separate the fabrics all round the edges as far as 12 mm ($\frac{1}{2}$ in.) inside the fitting line. Trim the turnings to 6 mm ($\frac{1}{4}$ in.) and fold them inside and slip-stitch the folded edges together all round.

2. Place the pockets in position on the garment and tack them. By hand, slip-stitch the pocket to the top layer only of the garment fabric, being very careful that no stitches show on the other side. This method is used when there is only one pocket on either side of the coat. If, however there are two hip level pockets on each side of the coat, they will lie exactly over each other, and it is possible though not very easy to machine them in place through all thicknesses.

Edges. The front edges and hems can be treated as described above for the pocket edges.

The more usual method is to bind the edges with woollen braid and pocket top hems can also be finished in this way.

Fold the braid not quite in half lengthwise and press the fold in.

On the coat, trim away the turnings to the fitting line and slip the raw edges inside the folded binding with the narrower side of the binding uppermost. Tack through all thicknesses along the edges of the binding,

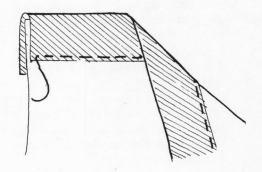

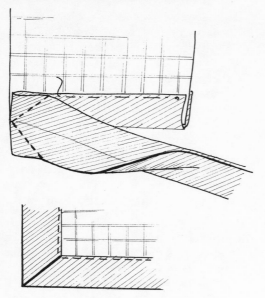

making sure that the underneath edge of the binding is caught in the tacking. Machine through the edges of the binding.

Wherever there is a corner the binding will have to be mitred as the diagram shows.

Collars.

1. Finish the outer edge in the chosen way (see Edges). When using binding and finishing the edge as in A in the diagram, insert the collar before applying the binding.
2. Trim the neck turnings of the collar to 6 mm ($\frac{1}{4}$ in.).
3. On the neck edge of the garment separate the two layers of fabric as far as 12 mm ($\frac{1}{2}$ in.) inside the fitting lines. Trim the turning allowance to 6 mm ($\frac{1}{4}$ in.).

4. Fold the turnings inside to the fitting lines and slip the raw edges of the collar between them so that all the fitting lines match. Tack and machine along the folded edges of the garment through all thicknesses.

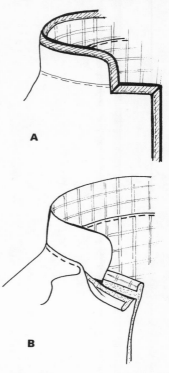

A

B

Note. When the fabric is bonded the collar will have to be attached with a welt seam.

Sleeves. Welt seams look best on raglan sleeves.

If it is necessary to put in a plain set-in sleeve, proceed as follows:

1. Cut the turning allowance of the armhole to 6 mm ($\frac{1}{4}$ in.) and separate the fabrics to a depth of 18 mm ($\frac{3}{4}$ in.) inside the fitting line. Fold the turnings to the inside on the fitting line, clipping across them round curved parts so that they will lie flat. Press well.

2. Trim the turnings of the sleeve to 9 mm ($\frac{3}{8}$ in.) and slip the raw edges between the folded edges of the arm-hole, easing in the surplus at the sleevehead. Tack in place. Using a glove mitt and a damp cloth shrink away the fullness round the head of the sleeve. Machine through the folded edges of the armhole.

Note. It would be unwise to attempt to put a plain sleeve into bonded fabric.

Fastenings. Only worked buttonholes are suitable. Frog fastenings and Velcro can be used. Open-ended zip fasteners can be used.

Single-breasted styles. Work the buttonholes on both fronts of the coat from the centre front line inwards. Sew buttons on the inner ends of the buttonholes as shown in the diagram.

Double-breasted styles. Work the buttonholes in the correct position down each front of the coat. The buttons are sewn on at the right-hand position only, back to back, see diagram.

Velcro. Tack and machine Velcro fastening to the front edges of the coat as shown in the diagram overleaf.

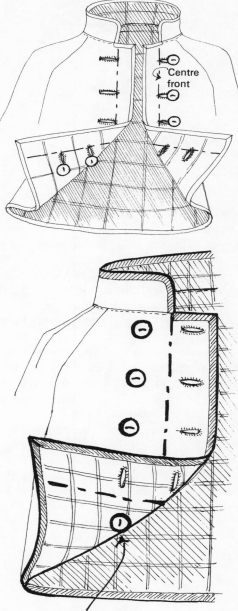

Buttons back to back

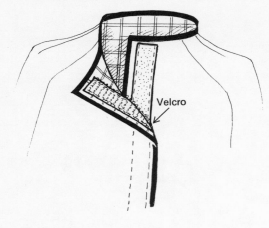

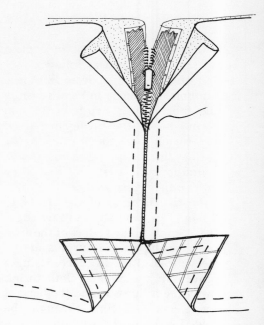

Zip fasteners.

1. For a front opening use an open-ended zip fastener.
2. Separate the fabrics down each front edge to a depth of about 18 mm ($\frac{3}{4}$ in.) or a little more. Fold the turnings to the inside on the fitting lines. Press well.
3. Insert the tapes of the zip fastener between the folded edges of the coat and tack in place down each side so that the edges of each front meet over the centre of the zip teeth.
4. Use a zipper foot on the machine and stitch 4 mm ($\frac{3}{16}$ in.) inside each edge through all thicknesses.

   If the zip does not reach to the bottom of the coat, slip-stitch the edges of the two fabrics to each other

below the zip to the hem. The top-stitching can then be carried right down to the hem if desired.

Pressing

This presents no difficulty. Press both sides under a damp cloth.

Cleaning

This fabric is not washable and requires dry-cleaning.

11. Metal thread and glitter fabrics

1. Some rich eastern silks have real metal thread, gold and silver, woven into them. These are beautiful fabrics but present making up problems.
2. The modern types of metal thread fabrics are made with Lurex woven or knitted into them. Lurex is wafer thin aluminium which may be gold, silver or coloured, sandwiched between two layers of transparent polythene which excludes the air and so prevents tarnishing.
3. All that glitters in fabric is not necessarily metal – sometimes polythene thread is introduced into fabric, causing it to glitter when the light catches it and to resemble metal thread.

REAL METAL THREAD FABRICS

These are not often met with today but are sometimes obtainable from abroad.
Width. Usually 91 cm (36 in.).
Uses. Evening dresses and coats.
Styles. If the fabric has a large pattern do not choose styles which are cut up into a lot of seams. These fabrics can be soft or really stiff and a design should be chosen to suit the weight and richness of the fabric.
Sewing thread. Pure sewing silk.
Hand-sewing needle. Sharps size 7 or 8.
Machine needle. Size 11 English or 70 Continental. Use a new one for each garment.

Underlining. Underlining gives a richness to the fabric and jap silk is suitable for the purpose.
Linings. Loose linings should also be made from jap silk.
Interfacing. Organdie or organza, which is the silk equivalent of organdie.

Problems

1. Metal thread blunts scissors.
2. These fabrics fray very readily.
3. Metal thread is scratchy and uncomfortable to the skin where it has cut ends as, for example, on seam turnings.
4. Silver metal thread tarnishes.
5. The machine needle coming straight down on a metal thread will pull it out of place and distort the pattern on the fabric.

Dealing with the Problems

1. Cut out with sharp scissors, even if they do have to be sharpened afterwards.
2. Cut the turnings wider than usual to allow for fraying, and iron strips of fusible fleece along the W.S. of the edges. This will hold the fraying threads in place.
3. All seam turnings should be neatened with binding which will enclose the

cut ends of the metal threads. Crossway strips of jap silk can be used for the binding.

All facings for necks and armholes should be cut from lining fabric rather than from the metal thread fabric itself.

The fabric looks richer when underlined and can have a loose lining as well, which will prevent most seams from being uncomfortably scratchy in wear.

4. Keep the garment wrapped in blue tissue paper when not in use. In the course of time it will tarnish but will still look attractive.

5. In the machine always use a fine, sharp, new needle, which is more likely to find its way between the threads of the fabric than to hit them during stitching.

Processes

Do not tailor tack as the threads will slip out of the fabric and removing them after stitching could damage the fibres. Trace out the fitting line with flat tacking.

Seams. Plain seams are the most suitable, neatened with crossway binding (see diagram on page 43).

Piped, overlaid and top-stitched seams can also be used.

Fastenings. There is no difficulty here as most types are suitable.

Hems. Neaten the raw edge of a hem with crossway binding and slip-stitch in place to the underlining.

Pressing

Press on the W.S. under a dry cloth. Never use any moisture, not even a steam iron, as this could cause the metal threads to tarnish.

Cleaning

These fabrics should always be dry-cleaned.

LUREX THREAD IN FABRICS

The basic fibre in the fabric may be anything from cotton, wool, rayons to synthetics, and the Lurex is woven or knitted into it.

Width. 91 cm (36 in.) to 150 cm (60 in.).
Uses. Cocktail and evening dresses and evening trouser suits.
Styles. Most styles are suitable, from those with soft drapery to the stiffer tailored designs.
Sewing thread. This will depend on the fibre from which the rest of the fabric is made. Use mercerised cotton for cottons and rayons, pure sewing silk for woollens and synthetic thread for synthetic fabrics.
Hand-sewing needles. Sharps size 7 or 8.
Machine needle. Size 11 English or 70 Continental.
Machine stitch. 12 stitches per 2·5 cm (1 in.) or setting 2 on a Continental machine.
Underlining & Linings. Use jap silk for woollen fabrics and fine taffeta or Tricel for rayons and synthetics.
Interfacing. Use organdie.

Problems

Sometimes fabrics with an all-over glitter of Lurex have a nap that glitters more when held up one way than the other.

The polythene coating on the metal is sensitive to heat and moisture.

Dealing with the Problems

1. Hang the fabric over something so that both cut ends are side by side and check for nap. If it has nap the pattern pieces must all be placed so that they run in the same direction. Nothing can be turned upside down for economical cutting.

2. For pressing always use a *cool* iron and a dry cloth on the W.S.

Cleaning

Lurex thread will wash or dry-clean, so the cleaning of the fabric depends on the fibre from which it is made.

GLITTER THREAD FABRICS

These can be treated as for fabrics with Lurex. The one thing to watch is the iron temperature, which should be *cool*, and do not use any moisture. When the fabric is washed see that it is quite dry before pressing and press on the W.S. as far as possible.

12. Allover sequinned fabric

This is a very difficult fabric to handle but when fashion dictates, it has to be used. A backing fabric is made by stitching horizontal rows of threads together with vertical rows of chain stitch in such a way that a checked pattern is formed consisting of alternate holes and blocks of threads as shown in the diagrams. On the right side rows of sequins are stitched in rather loosely.

Uses. The fabric can only be used for decorative bands, cuffs, yokes, and hem trimmings, and for simple shift-type dresses.

Width. 91 cm (36 in.).

Styles. Choose only straight loose dresses with just side seams and no darts because anything more complex would be almost impossible to make up. No set-in sleeves.

Sewing threads. Mercerised cotton size 40.

Hand-sewing needle. Size 8 sharps.

Machine needle. Size 11 English and 70 Continental.

Machine stitch. Use a small stitch to make sure of catching in the threads. 12–14 per 2·5 cm (1 in.). Dial 2–1½ on Continental sewing machines.

Interfacings. None.

Linings. Taffeta or Tricel types.

Problems

1. Cutting the plastic sequins can blunt scissors.

2. There are so many holes in the fabric that stitching and even tacking is difficult.
3. The sequins are sewn on so loosely that the fabric is inclined to shed them where it is cut.
4. The loose threads of the fabric tend to fray readily when cut.
5. The sequins are very scratchy and uncomfortable against the skin.
6. Machine stitching may perforate the sequins so that they split.

Dealing with the Problems

1. Do not use best scissors for cutting out.
2. Tack the horizontal threads with tiny stitches and use a fairly small machine stitch.
3, 4. Stick Sellotape along all edges immediately they are cut.
5. Garments should be mounted and also loose lined.
6. Take sequins from unwanted scraps of fabric and sew them on where others have split and fallen off.

Processes

Layout & cutting out. Lay the pattern on the underlining, cut out and trace the fitting lines on it with flat tacking. Place the sequinned fabric face downwards on the table and then lay the cut out underlining pieces onto the

W.S. of it. Pin and cut out the sequinned fabric, then baste-tack the two fabrics together. Now tack up the seams on the W.S. and fit the dress.

Seams. Only plain seams are possible. Try to tack them up so that the sequins match at the joins. This is most easily done if a row of sequins is removed from each turning just outside the fitting line. The checquered background that is left is then put together so that holes lie on top of holes and threads on top of threads. (In order to show this in the diagrams the underlining has not been drawn in and the fabric is shown as though it was unlined.) Now the garment is tacked up so that the rows of sequins on the R.S. just meet down the seam.

When the seam has been stitched, and this is really better done by hand although it is possible to machine it, there may be gaps on the R.S. showing the background but no sequins. When this happens, these gaps can be filled in by sewing on extra sequins from spare scraps of the fabric.

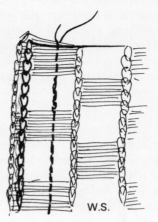

W.S.

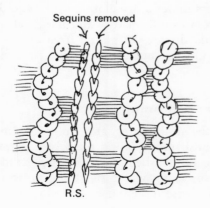

Sequins removed

R.S.

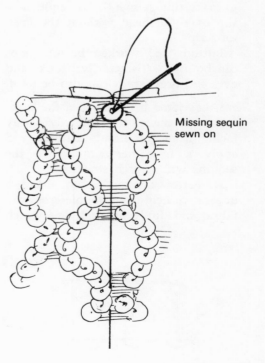

Missing sequin sewn on

On the W.S. unpick all the sequins off the turnings so that they will not be scratchy in wear. To neaten the seam turnings overcast or machine zig-zag the two fabrics together, press the seam open with a *cool* iron on the W.S. over a roller.

Facings. Cut these from the lining material. Armholes and necks should be faced for comfort, unless a loose lining is also used, in which case the turnings of the loose lining can be slip stitched to those of the garment.

Fastenings. The invisible type of zip could be used, but not in a centre back position where it would be stiff for the wearer to fasten. It would be best to make this garment loose enough to slip over the head without the need for a zip.

Buttons and worked button loops can be used satisfactorily. Hooks and eyes and press studs can also be used.

Hems. Level the hem and trim the turnings to 12 mm ($\frac{1}{2}$ in.). Cut a crossway facing from the lining material and apply a false hem, otherwise the sequins will scratch stockings.

A better method is to make a decorative hem from double crossway fabric and apply an underlay which

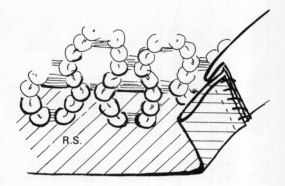

will show just below the sequin edge on the R.S. as the diagram shows.

Trimmings. These are best applied on top of a plain dress rather than inserted. Turnings can be kept to a minimum and unwanted sequins removed. Fold the turnings under, place the trimming in position on the dress and hem it firmly in place, taking the stitching just under the sequins so that it does not show on the R.S.

Pressing

Press under a dry cloth on the W.S. with a cool iron. Moisture and too much heat could distort the plastic from which the sequins are made.

Care & cleaning

If the underlining and lining are made from drip-dry fabric the whole garment can be washed carefully by hand in warm soapy water and hung up to dry. Otherwise it should be dry-cleaned.

False hem

These fabrics are neither woven nor knitted. The fibres, usually synthetic, are laid across each other in the required pattern and are needled together to hold them in place, often with a type of chain stitch. The fabrics can be bulky with an openwork effect or they can be fine and give the appearance of knitted fabric. It is the former type which presents sewing problems and is dealt with here.

Width. 91 cm (36 in.) to 137 cm (54 in.)
Uses. Tunics, day and evening dresses.
Styles. These should be simple with not too much detail, the fabric is decorative and provides the interest.
Sewing thread. Synthetic thread.
Hand-sewing needle. Size 8 sharps.
Machine needle. Size 11 English or 70 Continental.
Machine stitch. 12 per 2·5 cm (1 in.) or dial 2 on a Continental machine.

Problems

1. Fabric frays badly when cut.
2. The openwork nature of these fabrics makes them difficult to stitch inconspicuously.

Dealing with the Problems

1. Cut wide turnings and machine round them before making up the garment.
2. Underline the fabric, using taffeta or tricel lining for the purpose.

Processes

Tailor tacking is almost impossible, so the fitting line should be traced out on the underlining before tacking it to the top fabric.

Seams. Use plain seams and no top-stitching. Neaten the turnings with crossway binding as the fabric frays so much.

Hems. Bind the raw edge and slip hem it to the underlining.

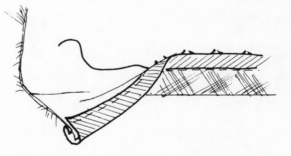

Facings. Whenever possible cut these from lining fabric.

Fastenings. Worked loops and buttons are the best solution. If it is necessary to use a zip fastener the opening must be faced with lining fabric before putting the fastener into the garment

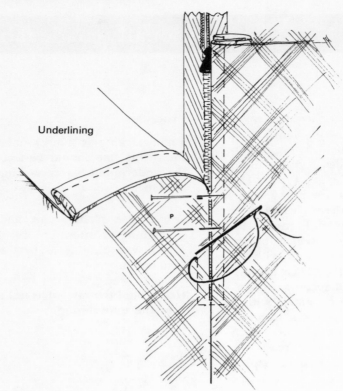

Underlining

or the loose fibres of the fabric will catch in the teeth of the zip. The fastener is best put in by hand.

Pressing

Use a pressing cloth and a cool iron and press on the W.S.

Cleaning

These fabrics usually wash well. Wash by hand and spin-dry. Iron W.S. out as the underlining will need pressing. Avoid catching the loose fibres of the fabric on rough edges during wear as they will pluck badly.

14. Net and lace

In former times many types of lace were made by hand with needle and thread or with bobbins on a pillow. Nowadays such work is only a hobby and net and lace are made commercially on machines. The structure is quite different from woven and knitted fabrics as the threads are twisted and tied round each other to form the net groundwork and the patterns worked into it.

The main types of lace the dressmaker can buy in the shops are:

Bobbin net made from nylon. This used to be made from cotton yarn, which was inflammable and dangerous.

Tulle, which is net made from silk and used mainly for bridal veils.

Flock-printed net, which has patterns printed on it with flock to look like velvet.

Lace, with embroidered patterns on net backgrounds made from cotton, rayon, nylon or silk, or a combination of any of these fibres.

Re-embroidered lace has a pattern outlined with heavy cord or has Lurex worked into it.

Guipure lace is a heavy type of machine embroidery worked on a background which is dissolved away after the embroidery has been completed. This is very expensive lace, costing several pounds a metre.

Uses. All these laces can be bought in the following forms:
1. Allover designs are wide dress laces used for dresses, blouses, lingerie, christening robes, stoles, collars and cuffs.
2. Wide nets used for ball gowns and veils.
3. Flouncing, which is wide lace with one straight 'selvedge' edge and the other a scalloped border. This is used for dresses.
4. Edgings have one straight edge and one scalloped one, used for trimmings.
5. Galon or galloon lace has both edges scalloped and is used for trimmings.
6. Insertion lace has two straight edges, and ribbon-hole insertion lace has slots through which ribbon can be threaded, both used for trimming. Small lace motifs can also be obtained for insertion.

Widths. Net 1·37 m (54 in.) wide, Tulle 1·83 m (72 in.) wide. Allover dress lace 0·9 m (34 in.–36 in.) wide. Occasionally 1·37 m (54 in.) wide. Flouncing 0·9 m (34 in.–36 in.) wide.

Styles. Choose styles for lace that are not cut up into panels which would spoil the beauty of the design on the lace.

Nets are usually used for ball gowns and are gathered layer upon layer to give a frothy effect. They are often embroidered with sequins, beads and rhinestones.

Threads to sew with. Mercerised cotton size 60. Machine embroidery cotton size 30.

Machine needle. Size 11 English, or 70 Continental.

Hand-sewing needle. Size 9.

Machine stitch length. 12 per 1·5 cm (1 in.) Singer or turn the dial to 2 on Continental machines.

Problems

1. Transparent, so all turnings will show through.
2. Delicate and open mesh – it is not easy to sew through holes.
3. Designs can be ruined by too elaborate a style, with a lot of seam lines.

Ways of dealing with the Problems

Underline allover dress lace. The underlining can be:

1. taffeta or poult in matching or contrasting colours,
2. net,
3. fine lawn or cotton fabric for underwear,
4. organdie, which adds a little stiffness but keeps the lace looking dainty. Choose simple styles with few seams.

Special Processes

Cutting out. Lace has no bias and pattern pieces may be cut along the length or across it. Study the design on lace and centralise it on the pattern pieces. This is most easily done by placing the paper pattern underneath the lace so that one can see exactly how the design can be arranged. Cut out any underlining separately.

When the lace is not to be underlined try to cut the seams so that the design can continue as though there was no join. This may cause a certain amount of wastage as extra turnings must be allowed so that they can be overlapped to match the design on the adjoining sections.

Underlining. Baste-tack the lace to the underlining all over to hold it firmly, starting down the centre and working outwards to the sides to prevent puckering. Keep the work flat on the table while tacking. The garment is then made up as if handling one fabric only.

Seams. When lace is underlined use plain seams, press them open and then overcast or zig-zag the raw edges to neaten. Lace does not fray but the underlining may unless it is net, and even then it is better to overcast them to hold the two layers of fabric together.

When lace is not underlined invisible seams may be made as follows:

Method 1

a. Lap the turnings of the two pieces to be joined over one another matching the design of the lace as far as possible. Tack in place.

b. The seam will not be straight but must be oversewn by hand or machined with a zig-zag stitch round the outline of the design as inconspicuously as possible.

c. Trim away the surplus turnings right down to the stitching.

Method 2

a. Lap the two pieces to be joined one over the other, matching the design.

Pin together along the outline of the design.

b. Trim the turnings of both sections to 6 mm ($\frac{1}{4}$ in.).

c. Stick the two sections together with fusible fleece. This makes the most invisible join of all and is quite strong.

Seams for net. Stitch a plain seam on the W.S. and trim the turnings to 6 mm ($\frac{1}{4}$ in.). Net does not fray so neatening is unnecessary and if the seams are pressed open and left as they are they will barely show on the R.S.

65

Frills. Measure the length of the edge to which the frill is to be attached and then cut the frill twice this length.

Raw edges. Necks and armholes can be finished with a binding or a facing of net. If the garment is underlined facings of the underlining fabric can be used. Crossway fabric bindings can be used for lingerie and nightwear and also narrow lace trimming which can be applied with a zig-zag machine or by whipping on by hand. Another method would be to finish a raw edge with the scallop pattern on a swing needle machine. Work the scalloped edge on the fitting line and then trim away the turnings.

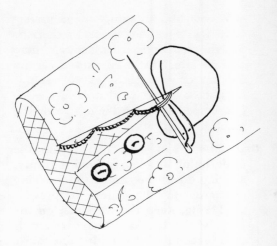

Fastenings. Buttonholes are not possible owing to the construction of the fabric but worked loops are ideal.

Small hooks and worked eyes and small press studs can be used. Zip fasteners are best used when the lace is underlined with fabric otherwise the tape will show through and look clumsy. They are best sewn in by hand.

Pockets. Only possible when the garment is underlined, when pockets inset in seams and patch pockets are suitable.

Lace underlined presents no problem. Level the hem and tack in place. Overcast or machine zig-zag the raw

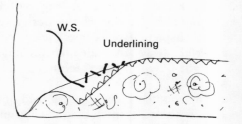

W.S.

Underlining

edges and slip hem to the underlining.

Lace unlined does present a problem and the best way to overcome this is to apply a false hem of net in a matching colour which will be practically invisible.

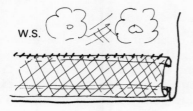

Hems. On net no hem is necessary; just trim the layers of net to the required length.

For a stiffened hem on unlined lace apply a horsehair braid:

1. Level the hem and trim leaving 6 mm ($\frac{1}{4}$ in.) turnings.
2. Just lap the edge of the braid over the hem turnings on the R.S. Tack and machine together as in the diagram.

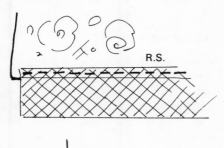

3. Turn the braid to the W.S. on the hem level line and slip hem as invisibly as possible to the lace.

Another way to give slight stiffness to a hem is to stick it in place with fusible fleece such as Bondina.

Flouncing has a finished scalloped edge but this can be given a stronger finish if a strip of net, folded double, is tacked behind the scallops which are then machined to the net as shown in the diagram.

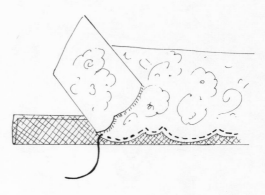

Sewing sequins on net.

1. Trace the design out on paper and tack it firmly behind the net.
2. Tack the outlines of the design to the net with coloured thread. Remove the paper.
3. Following the design, sew on the sequins making them touch or overlap so that the thread can be carried from one sequin to the next without showing through the net. Isolated sequins scattered here and there will have to be stitched on separately. (See diagrams overleaf for methods of stitching the sequins.)

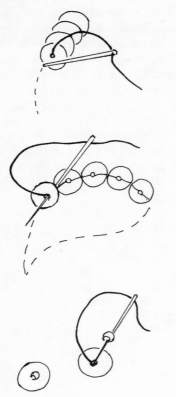

into the soft pad and press it without flattening it. It is always safer to press under muslin to avoid catching the toe of the iron in the delicate mesh of the lace, particularly when pressing guipure.

Care and laundering

It is essential to know the fibres from which the lace is made so that it can be given the correct treatment. Cotton, rayon, acetate and nylon lace can be washed gently in warm water with soap-flakes or detergents.

Lace made from silk is best dry-cleaned.

Heat can discolour, moisture can cause mildew, strong light can rot the lace and moths will attack wool and silk fibres, therefore garments made from lace should be hung up in a cool dry cupboard. When dresses are not going to be used for a while, pin tissue paper round them and slip them into a cotton bag made from an old sheet or even into plastic bags which can be fastened around the hook of the hanger with a rubber band.

Pressing

Use a cool iron, the setting depending on the fibre or fibres from which the lace is made.

Lace has a right and a wrong side, the design having a thicker outline on the R.S. Guipure lace has a heavy padded appearance on the R.S. and this must be retained. Place lace R.S. down on a clean cloth over thick felt or several layers of blanket and then press from the W.S. This will force the raised part of the lace

Mending tears in lace

Torn lace can be mended invisibly in the following way.
1. Cut a piece of net in a matching colour large enough to completely cover the area of the tear. Iron fusible fleece onto it.
2. Place the net to the W.S. of the lace and arrange the edges of the tear together over it. Fuse together by pressing with a hot iron over a damp cloth.

These include chiffon, georgette and organza (all made from silk fibres) and nylon chiffon, Terylene lawn, organdie (cotton) and many others, also transparent knits usually made from nylon.

Uses. Evening dresses, blouses, night-dresses and négligés, dressing gowns, and children's party dresses.

Organdie is useful for interlining and for underlining lace.

Sewing threads. For silk, use pure sewing silk.

For nylon and Terylene, use synthetic sewing threads.

For rayons and organdie, use mercerised cotton size 50 or machine embroidery cotton size 30.

Machine needle. Sizes 9 or 11 English or 70 Continental.

Hand-sewing needle. Size 9 sharps.

Size of Machine stitch 12 per 2·5 cm (1 in.) Singer, and on Continental machines turn the dial to 2. For knitted fabrics use the smallest possible zig-zag on a swing needle machine.

Widths. Vary from 0·91 m (36 in.) to 1·52 cm (60 in.).

Styles. Being so thin, light and billowy, most of these fabrics will gather very well and a metre (yard) could pull up into just a few centimetres (inches). Draped, swathed and frothy frilly styles are very suitable. Soft folds look good but not pleats unless they are permanent pleats put into synthetic fabric professionally. For these styles and those with a 'see through' look use only loose linings because underlining would destroy the light flimsy qualities of the fabrics. Underlinings can be used with sheer fabrics for more sculptured styles when they can be of matching or contrasting colours to gleam through the transparent fabrics. Sometimes a contrasting shade is very attractive when the sheer fabric has a printed design. Underlinings make the handling of sheer fabrics easier in many ways, particularly in helping the lighter fabric to retain its shape. Suitable underlinings would be jap silk for silk sheers, taffeta and tricel for synthetics and rayons, and nylon tricot for synthetic knits.

Problems

1. Most of these fabrics are so lightweight and slippery that they move about when being cut out.
2. Tailor tackings slip out.
3. The fabrics are made from very fine yarn, usually very closely woven, and machine stitching can cause the fabric to pucker because the needle, instead of finding its way between the threads of the fabric, comes straight down onto a thread making it tighten and pucker right across the fabric.

Also the fabric can bunch up in the feed dog of the machine and become damaged and plucked.

4. Transparency causes seam turnings, facings and hems to show through on the right side of the garment.

Ways of dealing with the Problems

1. Cover the cutting out table with sheets of tissue paper, stuck together to make one complete sheet. Place the fabric on top and straighten the grain lines, then pin it to the paper at frequent intervals along the edges. Place the paper pattern on the fabric and pin firmly, using sharp-pointed steel pins or needles, placing them within the turning allowance and taking them right through to the tissue paper underneath. Cut out with sharp scissors right through the fabric and tissue paper. In this way the pattern pieces will retain their correct shape.

2. Tailor tacking is not satisfactory for these fabrics; apart from the fact that tackings slip out of silky fabrics, they do not give a good guide to the fitting line on a fabric which moves about all over the place, constantly changing its shape. All the fitting lines should be traced on the fabric with flat tacking as follows:

   a. Tear away the tissue paper from under the fabric, leaving it just pinned to the pattern.

   b. As the fabric is transparent the fitting lines printed on the paper pattern should show through. Slip a finger between the two edges of the fabric and tack the outline of the fitting lines to the upper layer only. Turn the fabric over and carefully remove the paper pattern, pinning the two layers of fabric together again within the turning allowances and, following the lines of tacking on the underside, trace them on the upper layer. When the sheer fabric is to be underlined, the fitting lines are marked on the underlining only, in a slightly different way.

   a. Pin the pattern to the underlining along all the fitting lines, placing the pins rather close to each other. After cutting out, turn the pieces over so that the fabric is uppermost.

   b. Tack the fitting lines to the top layer of fabric only, along the pins. Take one pin at a time out of the pattern and replace it through the line of tacking on the top side, through both layers of fabric but *not* through the paper pattern. When all the pins have been transferred from underneath to the top, the fabric can be turned over and the paper pattern discarded.

   c. Following the lines of pins, trace the fitting lines on the second side.

3. Always use a new machine needle when stitching these fabrics and the finest that can be threaded with the sewing thread you are using. Place tissue paper between the feed dog and the fabric to prevent plucking and bunching up. The paper can be torn away afterwards. When stitching knitted fabrics on a swing needle machine,

use the slightest possible zig-zag, setting the dial or lever only just off the straight position.

4. When the sheer fabric is underlined there is no problem, but when it is used as a 'see through' fabric, seam turnings and hems must be as inconspicuous as possible.

Processes

Tacking up. Place the fitting lines exactly together and put a pin at each end across the seam turning, then, if one edge of the fabric appears to have stretched slightly in the handling, it can be coaxed back to lie flat along the length of the seam. Use fine tacking cotton and tack the seam with very small tacking stitches.

Seams. For dresses, place the R.S. of the fabric together and pin, tack and stitch along the fitting lines. Trim the turnings to 3 mm ($\frac{1}{8}$ in) and either blanket-stitch them together or use the zig-zag on a swing needle machine.

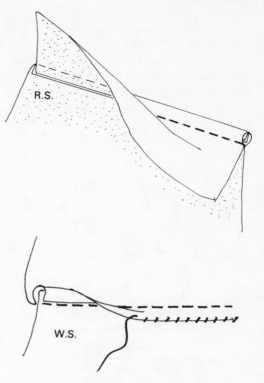

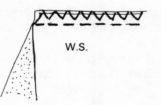

For blouses, dressing gowns and children's party dresses, use a tiny French seam 3 mm ($\frac{1}{8}$ in.) deep.

For nightdresses use a machine and fell seam 3 mm ($\frac{1}{8}$ in.) wide.

Darts. It is important that any fastening off of the thread should not show through at the pointed end and this can be avoided by stitching the dart as follows:

1. Thread the machine up but do not thread the needle.
2. Take the bobbin thread where it comes through the hole in the throat plate and thread it through the needle in the opposite direction from the way the top cotton would be threaded and pull it through for twice the length of the dart plus about 10 cm (4 in.).

3. Knot the end of the bobbin thread to the top thread.
4. Wind the thread back onto the reel until the knot is pulled up and the thread is taut in the needle.
5. Starting at the pointed end, proceed to stitch the dart, taking the first four stitches along the fold before gradually widening out.

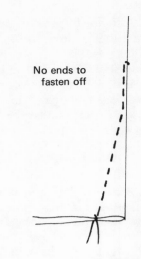

No ends to fasten off

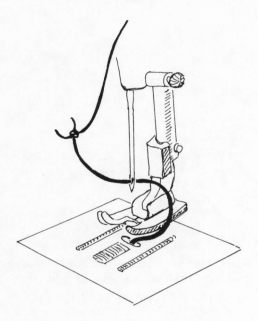

Fastenings. Piped or bound buttonholes are not possible because the turnings would show through and look ugly.

Worked buttonholes can be used where organdie would be suitable for an interfacing, for example on Terylene lawn.

Rouleau and worked loops would be the most suitable button fastenings.

Small hooks and worked eyes can be used and small press studs are permissible provided they do not fasten so tightly that pulling them apart damages the fabric.

Zip fasteners can be used on Terylene lawn and underlined garments but even polyester zips are too heavy on really sheer fabrics.

Edges. Armhole and neck edges can be bound with crossway fabric. This is most easily done if the binding is double, the fabric being thin enough to allow this.

1. Cut the crossway strip six times the required finished width. Fold in half lengthwise with the R.S. outside.
2. Trim the turning allowance of the garment right away to the fitting line. (If the fabric frays badly, e.g. nylon chiffon, do not cut away the turnings until after the binding has been machined in place.)

3. Place the folded binding to the R.S. of the garment with the raw edges along the fitting line. Tack and machine one third of the depth of the binding below the raw edges. *Note.* Around concave curves the binding must be stretched slightly and around convex ones eased so that it may lie flat.
4. Press the binding up and turn the folded edge over to the W.S. so that it lies along the machine stitching. Tack in place.
5. Hem the folded edge of the binding to the machine stitching.

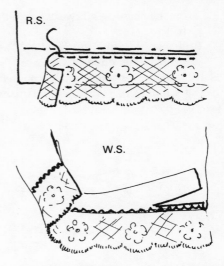

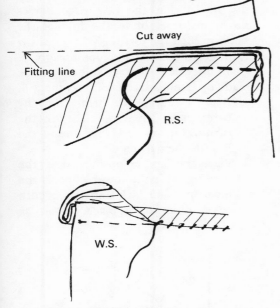

2. Machine along the inner edge of the lace.
3. Fold the garment turnings to the W.S. clipping across them around a curved edge.
4. From the R.S. work machine zig-zag over the edge of the lace and through the folded under-turnings. (Stitch width 1½–2, stitch length 1 or less.)
5. On the W.S. trim the turnings right down to the stitching.

If no swing needle machine is available put the lace on as follows:
1. Tack the lace to the garment with the R.S. together and the straight edge of the lace along the fitting line.

Edges can be trimmed with lace as follows:
1. Place the lace on the turnings on the R.S. of the garment with the inner edge along the fitting lines and tack in place.

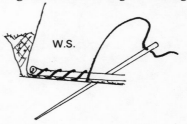

2. Trim the turning allowance to 6 mm ($\frac{1}{4}$ in.).
3. Roll the turning to the W.S. and whip it to the edge of the lace.

Frills can be applied with crossway facing 9 mm ($\frac{3}{8}$ in.) wide when finished (see diagram).

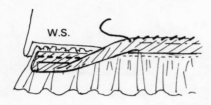

Hems. Hang the garment up overnight before attempting to level it in order to let it drop and relax and find its own level.

A narrow rolled hem is very suitable as it is almost invisible.

1. Level the hem, marking it with a line of tacking.
2. Trim the turnings to 6 mm ($\frac{1}{4}$ in.) and press it over to the W.S. 3 mm ($\frac{1}{8}$ in.) below the level line.
3. Working on the W.S., take a stitch in the fold and then pick up one thread only of the garment on the level line. Continue in this way

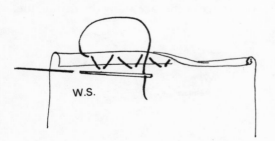

pulling the thread taut as the work proceeds so that the turning rolls over to the level line enclosing the raw edges.

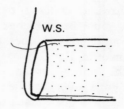

When a deep hem is required, as on children's clothes, make it completely double so that the raw edge comes down inside right to the fold at the bottom, then the turning will not show through on the R.S. and look unsightly.

On lingerie an attractive hem can be made by using a lace facing on the R.S.

1. After levelling the hem, trim the turnings to 3 mm ($\frac{1}{8}$ in.). Press the turning up on the level line to the R.S. of the garment.
2. Place the lace in position over the turning with the lower edge to the level line and tack and stitch both edges of the lace in place.

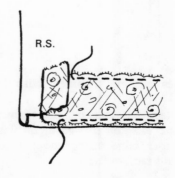

A hem can also be finished with a frill.

1. Level the hem, trim the turning to 3 mm ($\frac{1}{8}$ in.) and press up onto the R.S.
2. Cut the frill twice as long as the hem is wide by twice the required depth and join in a circle.
3. Press the raw edges of the frill to the W.S. so that they just meet along the centre. Work a gathering row 3 mm ($\frac{1}{8}$ in.) either side of the raw edges.
4. Pull up the frill to fit the hem and tack in place as shown in the diagram. Machine the frill to the hem along each gathering line.

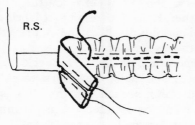

A shell edge hem is another suitable method for lingerie.

1. Tack up a hem on the W.S. 3 mm ($\frac{1}{8}$ in.) deep.
2. Work three small running stitches through the top edge of the hem

and then take one blanket stitch right over the edge of the hem and pull it tight, as shown in the diagram.

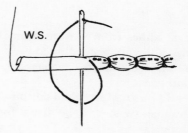

Pressing

Always use a cool iron and press under dry muslin. The temperature of the iron depends on the fibre from which the fabric is made. Avoid using moisture at all times on silk sheers which absorb moisture and the extra weight of this can cause the hem to drop and change the behaviour of the fabric.

Cleaning

Organdie and synthetic sheers will usually wash quite easily. Silk sheers should be dry-cleaned.

16. Leather and suede

Leather comes from various animals and the size will vary according to the animal.

Uses. Jackets, skirts, waistcoats, hats, trimmings etc.

Thread to use. Mercerised cotton size 40. Buttonhole twist can be used for top-stitching.

Hand-sewing needle. Use three-sided gloving needles.

Machine needle. Special three-sided machine needles are made for leather.

Size of machine stitch. 6 to 7 stitches per 2·5 cm (1 in.) for Singer machines and for Continental machines dial $2\frac{1}{2}$ or 3.

If possible use a roller foot on the machine as this makes stitching much easier.

Adhesive. Upholstery or rubber solution.

Problems

1. The skin is irregular in shape and is only the size of the animal from which it comes and parts of it may be unusable. Suede has a pile which smooths one way only.
2. All pin and needle perforations show.
3. Leather is tough to sew.

Dealing with the Problems

Choice of pattern. A style made up of small sections is best as it fits more economically into the skins. This means that larger sections of a garment, e.g. skirts, often have to be joined to obtain the required length and width and these joins can be turned into decorative features such as yokes and top-stitched seams. As alterations are hard to disguise, make sure that the pattern fits the wearer. It is safer to run it up in some cheap material or in odd bits one may have, to check the fit before cutting up the leather, bearing in mind that fabric drapes and moulds itself to the figure whereas leather is less supple.

Preparation of leather. Check for thin places and holes and mark round them with tailor's chalk on the W.S. so that they can be avoided when planning the layout. On suede skins mark the direction of the pile on the W.S. with arrows indicating the way it smooths downwards as pattern pieces cannot be turned upside down for economical cutting.

Layout. Lay all pattern pieces on the W.S. of the skin and plan all of them before cutting any of them out, so that they can be arranged with the minimum wastage. On suede skins watch that the pile smooths downwards on all pattern pieces. The stretch of a skin usually runs round the animal rather than down the length, so that the larger pattern pieces should be placed with the 'grain' running from head to tail and vice versa. As far as possible sections which will get the most wear, such as the backs of skirts, should be placed on the thickest parts of the skin. Arrange small, less important pieces, such as insides of pockets and piping for buttonholes, on the thinner edges of the skin which stretch more easily.

After arranging pattern pieces, keep them in place with weights, for they cannot be pinned. Chalk the outline of the pattern *very accurately* and chalk in all balance marks. Now fold back the turning allowances of the pattern to the fitting lines, clipping across the paper at intervals around curved parts, such as necks and armholes, to enable the turnings to fold back flat, and chalk the fitting lines on the skin. When part of a pattern piece has to be placed to a fold, chalk one side and mark in the line which has to go on a fold and then turn the pattern over on this line and chalk the other side, because leather cannot be cut double.

Cutting out. Cutting leather with scissors, however sharp, can be hard work – a really sharp knife is easier to use provided something to protect the table is placed under the skin.

Assembling. Seam turnings can be held together with slip-on paper clips or with masking tape on the W.S. Place the fitting lines together accurately because alterations cannot be made after stitching as all pin and needle marks will show and cannot be erased.

Sewing. Use three-sided needles and a roller foot on the machine which glides easily over the thick leather. Try to avoid the R.S. of the leather coming into contact with the feed on the machine as it may stick and not feed through properly, and anyway it would mark it.

Processes

Types of seam. Plain seams pressed open or top-stitched. Closed welt seams. Overlaid top-stitched seams.

Plain seams.
1. Hold the two pieces to be joined together with masking tape or with paper clips at frequent intervals. The tape is best because clips could mark the fabric.
2. Machine together along the fitting lines.
3. Open the seam out (curved seams will have to be clipped across at intervals to enable them to lie flat). Press carefully with a warm iron.
4. Thick skins will have to be hammered gently to flatten the seams.
5. When the skin is thick, pare away some of the edge along the underside of the turnings to thin them out.
6. Using upholstery or rubber solution, stick the turnings to the garment, gently hammering them flat.

For a plain top-stitched seam proceed as above and then on the R.S. machine the required width away from the seam.

Closed welt seams.
1. Stitch the seam as for a plain seam as far as 2.

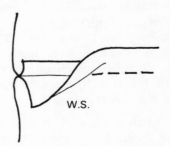

W.S.

2. Trim down one side of the turnings to 3 mm ($\frac{1}{8}$ in.) and fold the wider turning over it. See diagram on page 77.
3. On the R.S. machine the required distance from the seam join so that the trimmed edge is enclosed, giving a padded effect.

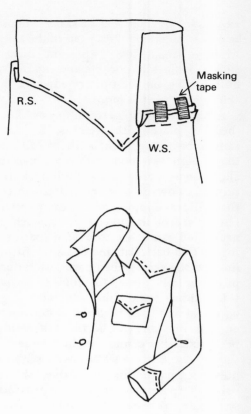

Overlaid top-stitched seam.
1. If the leather is thick pare down the turnings of the top section to thin them.
2. Fold these turnings to the W.S. on the fitting line and hammer gently on the W.S. They could be fixed down with adhesive.

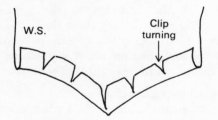

3. Lap this section over the turnings of the one to which it is to be joined, matching the fitting lines. The two sections will have to be held together with the masking tape on the W.S.
4. With the R.S. uppermost stitch the two sections together.

Darts. Stitch as for a plain seam and slit open down the centre of the fold.

Flatten out and top-stitch or stick down with adhesive. *Alternative method:* Before stitching cut down the centre of the dart to the point. Overlap the cut edges until the fitting lines meet and then stitch straight down the centre to the point. Trim away the dart turning allowance on the R.S. to the stitching.

Fastenings. Interfacings are unnecessary as the leather is strong enough without them and they would add bulk to a bulky fabric.

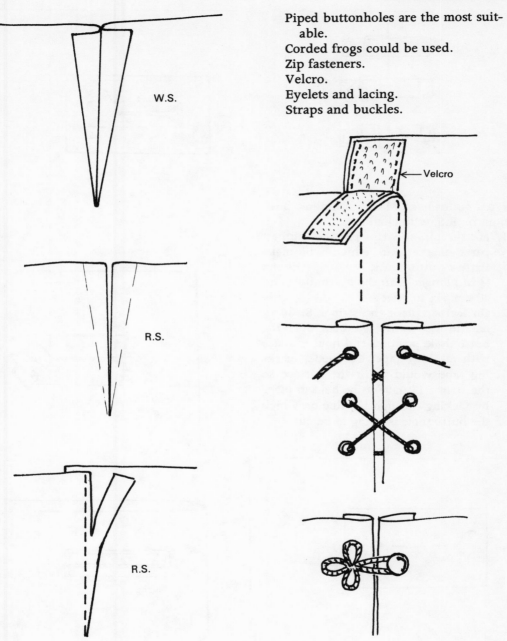

W.S.

R.S.

R.S.

Piped buttonholes are the most suitable.
Corded frogs could be used.
Zip fasteners.
Velcro.
Eyelets and lacing.
Straps and buckles.

Velcro

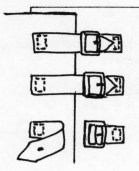

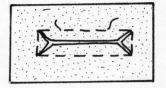

Piped buttonholes. Mark buttonhole positions on R.S. with chalk.

1. For the piping strips use the thinnest parts of the skin which will make flattest buttonholes. Cut strips 19 mm ($\frac{3}{4}$ in.) longer than the buttonhole and 40 mm ($1\frac{1}{2}$ in.) deep.
2. On leather place the strip R.S. down on the R.S. of the garment over the buttonhole position and hold in place with masking tape. On suede, masking tape would mark the surface so the strip will have to be held in place by tacking through the line on which the buttonhole is going to be cut.

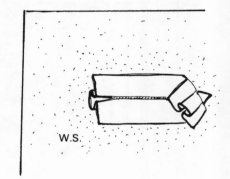

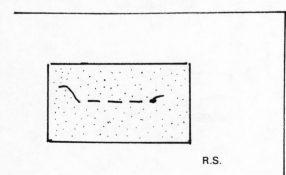

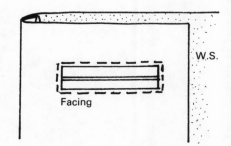

3. Machine 3 mm ($\frac{1}{8}$ in.) either side of the buttonhole mark and across each end, starting in the centre of one side and ending up by overlapping a few stitches in order to avoid having to fasten off the thread.

4. Cut the strip, mitring each end and turn the strip through to the W.S.

5. On the R.S. form an even piping and stick it down on the W.S. with adhesive, hammering it gently.

6. Fold the facing in position and on the R.S. of the garment machine all round the buttonhole immediately outside the piping and through all thicknesses. Before stitching place tissue paper between the feed-dog of the machine and the garment to prevent the facing from being damaged.

7. Through the lips of the buttonhole from the R.S. cut a slit in the facing and then cut away that part of the facing which lies over the piping just inside the oblong of machine stitching.

Button moulds. These can be covered with leather using the thinnest parts of the skin only. If the skin is too thick, pare it down on the underside.

Zip fasteners. Either stab-stitch in by hand or put in by machine using a zipper foot, in which case the zip tapes will have to be held firmly in place with masking tape on the W.S.

1. Fold the turnings of the opening to the W.S. and stick them down with adhesive and hammer flat from the W.S. Draw the folded edges together with masking tape.

2. On the W.S. of the garment place the zip centrally over the seam and hold this in place with masking tape.

3. On the R.S., using a zipper foot, machine 5 mm ($\frac{3}{16}$ in.) in from the fitting lines either side of the zip teeth. Stitch twice across the base. See diagrams overleaf.

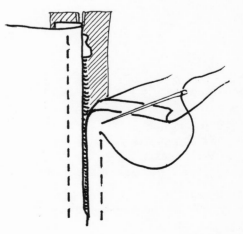

M.M.I.N.—F

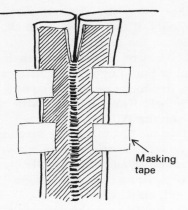

W.S.

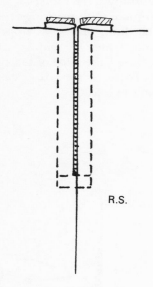

R.S.

gently on W.S. Wedge shaped pieces will have to be trimmed out of the turnings of convex curves so that they will lie flat and the turnings of concave curves will have to be snipped across.

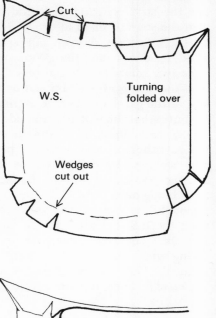

Cut

W.S.

Turning folded over

Wedges cut out

Masking tape

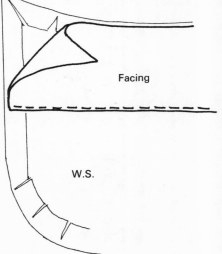

Facing

W.S.

Pockets include –
    Patch pockets,
    Welt pockets,
    Those cut as part of the garment.

Patch pocket.
1. Fold all the turnings to the W.S. and fix down with adhesive and hammer

2. Cut a top facing for the pocket hem without any turnings. Place in position on the inside of the pocket and stitch the lower and top edges to the pocket as in the diagram.
3. Hold the pocket in place on the R.S. of the garment with masking tape. On suede the tape will have to go inside the pocket like a stamp hinge to avoid it marking the fabric where it will show.
4. Stitch the pocket in place carefully because rectified mistakes will always show.

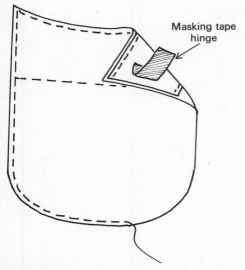

Masking tape hinge

Welt pocket.
1. Choose a thin part of the skin from which to cut the welt and cut it the exact length required by twice the depth plus 9 mm ($\frac{3}{8}$ in.) for a turning.
2. Cut out two sections for the pocket bag in lining fabric, making each piece 2·5 cm (1 in.) wider than the welt and 15 cm (6 in.) deep.

3. Take one pocket bag piece and fold the top edge over to the W.S. for 9 mm ($\frac{3}{8}$ in.) and press it well. With the W.S. uppermost place one long edge of the welt over the folded back turning of the lining section so that the extra width of the lining is arranged equally at either end of the welt. Machine the two together as shown in the diagram.
4. Face the top edge of the inner pocket section on the R.S. with a strip of leather 5 cm (2 in.) deep. Stitch along the lower edge of the leather only.

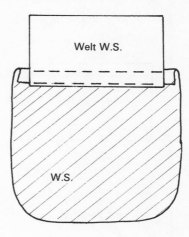

Welt W.S.

W.S.

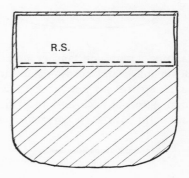

R.S.

83

5. On the R.S. of the garment mark the pocket mouth position with chalk. Place the free edge of the welt, W.S. uppermost, immediately below the chalk line. Place the inner pocket bag R.S. down above the pocket mouth mark.

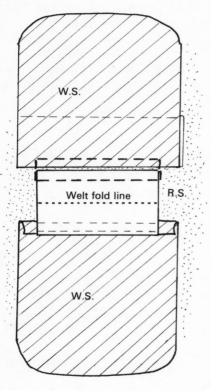

6. Machine 3 mm ($\frac{1}{8}$ in.) either side of the pocket mark and across each end.
7. Cut along the pocket mark to within 6 mm ($\frac{1}{4}$ in.) of each end and then cut diagonally into each corner.

8. Push the pocket pieces through the slit to the W.S. Fold the welt over for the required depth and machine *through the folded welt only* along the actual seam line where it joins the garment. Turn the welt up onto the garment and machine across each end twice to hold it in place, as in the diagram.

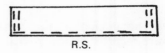

9. On the W.S. tack the two pocket pieces together and, with the pocket down on the machine and the garment uppermost, stitch the two pieces together. Neaten the raw edges with machine zig-zag stitch or with blanket stitch.

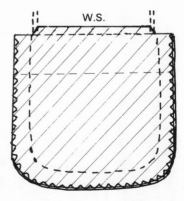

Pocket cut as part of the garment.
1. Cut the inner pocket section in lining fabric 15 cm (6 in.) square.
2. Place in position on the lower part of the garment with the R.S. together

and hold with paper clips or masking tape. Machine together 9 mm ($\frac{3}{8}$ in.) below the top edges for the exact width of the pocket, i.e. 12·5 cm (5 in.) leaving 12 mm ($\frac{1}{2}$ in.) turnings either side on the lining.

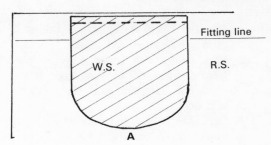

Fitting line

W.S.   R.S.

A

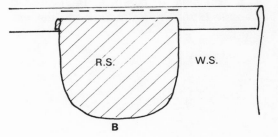

R.S.   W.S.

B

3. Fold the pocket section and the turnings of the leather over to the W.S. on the fitting line.
4. On the R.S. top stitch along the top edge of the pocket for its exact length.
5. Place the lower part of the garment over the top part on the R.S., matching the fitting lines, and hold in place with masking tape. Top stitch the two sections together either side of the pocket topstitching.
6. On the W.S. stitch the pocket bag pieces together.

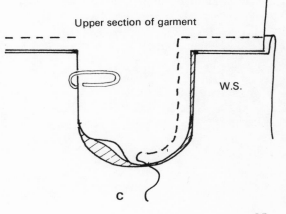

Upper section of garment

W.S.

C

85

Hems

1. Level the hem with a chalk line and trim to the required depth.
2. Pare down the inner edge of the hem to thin it out and stick it up onto the garment with upholstery solution.
3. On the W.S. hammer the hem gently to flatten the fold.

When a garment has a flared hem it is best to make it only 6 mm ($\frac{1}{4}$ in.) deep and top stitch it in place.

If a deeper hem is required on a flare it will have to be slit at intervals *not quite to the fold of the hem,* to dispose

of the surplus material. The reason for cutting the slit not quite to the base of the fold is that it is very easy to make the hem pointed at the base of a slit instead of a smooth curve. Cut away

just enough leather on either side of each slit to enable the edges to meet when stuck down.

Inserting a lining in a jacket or coat

1. Make up the jacket completely, and stick the hem in place.
2. Make up the lining.
3. Place the R.S. of the lining to the R.S. of the jacket and tack and machine the lining to the facings of the jacket, starting from the hem, up one front, round the neck and down the other front.
4. Turn R.S. out.
5. Turn up the hem of the lining, making it 2·5 cm (1 in.) shorter than the jacket and slip hem it in place to the jacket. This is most easily worked with the jacket inside out on a dummy or a coat hanger.

PVC sheeting is entirely plastic and water-proof and is not in the strict sense a fabric but is stitched up into articles and garments.

Uses. Sponge bags, blanket bags, hanging shoe and handbag slings, hanging wardrobes, raincoats and hoods, and shower curtains.

Width. Obtainable in various widths — and also in varying densities.

Styles. Choose raincoat patterns with raglan sleeves as set-in sleeves are difficult to handle.

Machine needles. 11 English, 80 Continental.

Hand-needles. Sharps size 7, but seldom used for this sheeting.

Thread. Sylko size 40.

Problems

1. All punctures made by pins and needles remain permanently. It is therefore impossible to pin or tack parts together.
2. Too strong a sewing thread might cut through the sheeting.
3. Sticks in the machine and is easily marked by the feed-dog.
4. Sheeting is not strong and may tear easily where it has been perforated by machine stitching. Edges are weak.

Ways of dealing with the Problems

1. Hold pattern pieces in position on the sheeting, prior to cutting out, with slip-on paper clips or with larger spring paper clips along the edges of the sheeting and with weights elsewhere.

   Chalk or pencil the outline of the pattern onto the PVC, remove the clips and pattern and cut out accurately along the pencilled lines. This is a more accurate method than cutting round the pattern which may slip out of position. After cutting, the fitting lines can be pencilled in lightly inside the cut edge for the depth of the turning allowance. Use a card marker to do this accurately.

   Avoid tacking or pinning by holding together sections which have to be

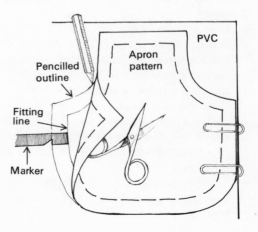

Pencilled outline

Apron pattern

PVC

Fitting line

Marker

joined with small pieces of Sellotape or with slip-on paper clips, prior to stitching. With garments such as raincoats when fitting is necessary, use Sellotape rather than clips, which may fall off.

Never tack and *never* pin, as unnecessary perforations weaken the sheeting.

2. Never use a synthetic sewing thread. These are fine and strong and could cut through the sheeting.

3. Spray the feed-dog of the sewing machine with an aerosol silicone spray which will help to prevent the sheeting sticking and not feeding through.

   Alternatively, place tissue paper between the feed-dog and the sheeting while stitching. This can be torn away afterwards and will stop the teeth of the feed-dog from marking the sheeting.

   Use a presser foot with a Teflon coating (some firms, e.g. Bernina, make these) or a special roller presser foot which rolls over the sheeting helping it to glide through the machine easily.

4. Use a long machine stitch, i.e., 8 stitches to 2·5 cm (1 in.) on Singer machines and on Continental machines set the stitch length dial to $2\frac{1}{2}$ or 3, so that the minimum number of perforations may be made.

   Use a fine machine needle, English size 11 or Continental size 80, so that the holes made may be as small as possible.

   Whenever possible strengthen the outside edges with straight or bias binding.

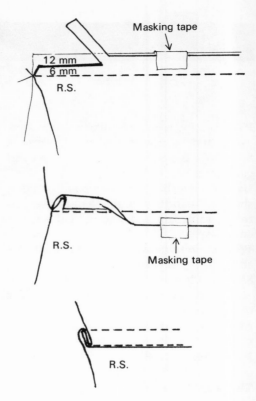

Suitable processes

Seams. For raincoats or hoods use double-stitched or welt seams.

Edges. Gathered or pleated frills may be put around the edges of aprons. When PVC is lightweight and flexible it is possible to gather it with running stitches 3 mm ($\frac{1}{8}$ in.) long which, when pulled up will make the frill.

1. To make a pleated frill, cut a strip the required depth plus 6 mm ($\frac{1}{4}$ in.) and three times the required length. Fold the pleats fixing them down with

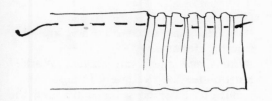

a strip of Sellotape placed just *inside* the fitting line so that it will not be caught in the stitching.

2. With the right sides together, place in position along the edge of the apron with clips or Sellotape.

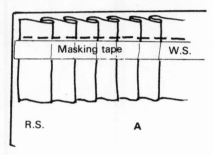

Masking tape W.S.

R.S. **A**

3. Machine together along the fitting line.
4. Remove the Sellotape and fold the seam turnings towards the garment on the W.S.

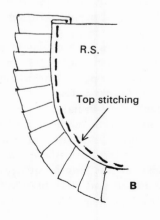

R.S.

Top stitching

B

5. On the R.S., top-stitch around the edge of the apron to hold the seam turnings in place and to give added strength.

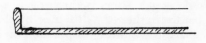

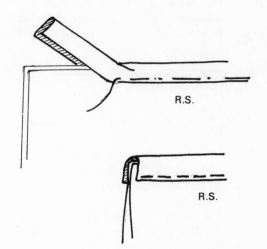

R.S.

R.S.

Binding edges or seam turnings. The raw edges of storage bags and hanging wardrobes can be neatened and strengthened by being enclosed in straight binding.

1. Fold the binding not quite in half lengthwise so that one side is a fraction longer than the other and press the crease in well.
2. Stitch the seam on the right side of the article and slip the raw edges inside the binding with the shorter side of the binding uppermost.
3. In this instance it is possible to tack the binding in place with long stitches.

89

4. Machine along the edges of the binding from the short side making sure that the longer underside is caught in the stitching.

Single edges, such as those of aprons, can be strengthened with bias binding.

1. Place the binding in position on the R.S. and tack with long stitches, a quarter of the depth of the binding down from the top edge. Machine in place.

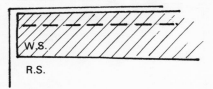

2. Turn the seam turnings up onto the binding.
3. Fold over the top raw edge of the binding to meet the other raw edges.
4. Fold binding over again to the W.S. and hem the folded edge to the machine stitches, *not* to the sheeting or too much perforation will occur.

Alternatively, apply the binding with the special binding foot on a sewing machine all in one operation.

Pockets. Patch pockets are the most suitable type.

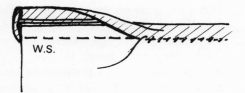

Fastenings.
Press studs are often used and are very suitable and strong.
Buttons and piped buttonholes. (Worked buttonholes are definitely impossible).

Buttons must be stitched through the sheeting onto a small button at the back so that no strain comes on the sheeting.

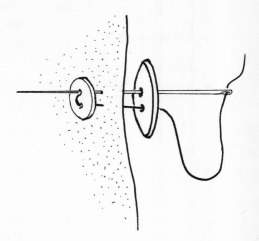

A piped buttonhole is worked as follows:

1. Pencil the buttonhole position on the sheeting.
2. Cut two pieces of the plastic for the lips of the buttonhole, 2·5 cm (1 in.) longer than the pencilled button mark by 13 mm ($\frac{1}{2}$ in.) wide.
3. Fold each piece in half lengthwise and place on the R.S. of the garment with the cut edges facing and touching each other along the buttonhole mark, and with the surplus length equally distributed either end. Fix in place with adhesive tape. (A)

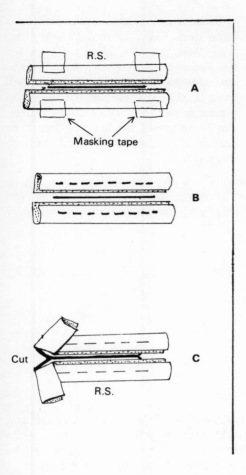

R.S.

A

Masking tape

B

Cut

C

R.S.

7. On the W.S. stitch the small triangles at each end of the slit to the ends of each strip.
8. Fold the facing under into position and, from the R.S., pencil through the opening to mark the place where the facing is to be cut.
9. Cut the slit in the facing, mitring each end. Fold the turnings under and machine very carefully along the folded edges all round the buttonhole, which should look exactly the same on both the right and wrong sides.

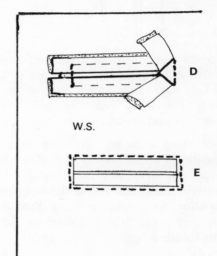

D

W.S.

E

4. Machine *exactly* along the centre of each folded strip, for the exact length of the buttonhole. (B)
5. Cut along the pencil line from the centre to within 3 mm ($\frac{1}{8}$ in.) of each end and then cut diagonally into each corner as far as the stitching. (C)
6. Pull the strips through the slit to the W.S. so that the folded edges now touch each other in the centre. Finger press.

Zip fasteners can be used and should be stitched in by machine rather than by hand. Bear in mind that if the PVC is transparent the tape of the zip does look rather heavy and will show through the sheeting. This matters only in a garment and is of no consequence when articles like blanket bags are being made.

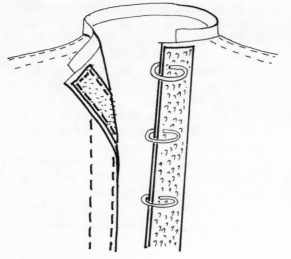

Bathroom and shower curtains could have deep hems to make them hang well. Turn the hem up on the W.S. for the required depth and machine the cut edge to the curtain. Curtains will have a similar hem at the top and plastic hooks, into which the PVC clips, can be obtained for hanging them; or curtain rods can be threaded through the top hem.

Belts. Tubular belts will not turn out, so the turnings have to be folded in and then placed together and top-stitched.

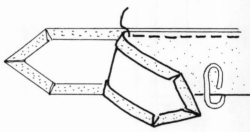

Pressing

This is not possible as the heat of the iron would melt the fabric. Seams can be flattened out with the fingers or can be placed under heavy books for a time.

Velcro is most useful as a fastener down the front of a raincoat, for a belt or for blanket bags and apron straps. It is merely placed in position, held with paper clips and machined along each edge.

Hems. Deep hems are not used for garments, as a rule. Using a hem marker level the hem and cut the sheeting away 6 mm ($\frac{1}{4}$ in.) below the level line, to allow for a small turning. Fold this turning to the W.S. and machine along the folded edge.

These fabrics are of two types: Plain or printed cotton fabric coated with clear PVC film and a soft thicker vinyl on a knitted cotton backing. Being thicker, the latter type is often textured by having a pattern embossed on it.

Widths. These vary from 0·91 m (36 in.) to 1·8 m (72 in.).

Uses. Raincoats, hoods and hats, waterproof aprons, wipe-down tablecloths, blanket bags, shopping bags, garden and car cushion covers and upholstery coverings.

Styles. Choose styles with raglan type sleeves as it is almost impossible to dispose of the surplus fabric at the head of a plain sleeve. Top-stitched styles are most suitable, slightly loose and belted, or flared styles because there is not much 'give' in the fabric and anything tight might be uncomfortable to wear. The vinyl bonded fabrics are more supple and likely to be more comfortable than the PVC film type. The fewer seams there are in a raincoat, the more waterproof it will be because rain trickles through the holes of the stitching.

Threads to use. Mercerised cotton size 40.

Machine needle. Size 14 English, 80 Continental.

Size of machine stitch. 8 stitches per 2·5 cm (1 in.) stitch length 3 on Continental machines.

Hand-sewing needle. Betweens size 7.

Problems

1. Pins and needles make permanent marks. Alterations show.
2. When stretched tightly, some of the printed, coated cottons lose a certain amount of colour density which is never regained.
3. When machine stitching on the R.S. fabric sticks badly between the needle and the throat plate and will not feed through.
4. Turned out edges, e.g. collars, tend to have a rolled appearance.
5. The fabric is dense and there is no ventilation through it.
6. Water runs off aprons onto one's feet.

Ways of dealing with the Problems

1. Use slip-on paper clips and weights to hold the paper pattern in place during cutting out, or pin in place within the turning allowance where any holes made by the pins will not show on finished garments.
   Note. It is better to place the pattern pieces on the W.S. of the fabric so that the fitting lines can be marked on the back more easily.
2. Avoid stretching the fabric in any way.
3. Either
   a. Oil the presser foot, throat plate and needle with machine oil. The dis-

advantage of this is that the thread gets oily and will pick up dirt and the sewing machine has to be thoroughly cleaned and left free from oil afterwards.

b. Sprinkle the fabric with French chalk or talcum powder.

c. Replace the presser foot with a roller foot which just rolls over the fabric and feeds it through without any trouble.

4. Top-stitch all turned out edges and this will keep them flat.

5. Put eyelet holes in raincoats under the arms for ventilation.

6. Stitch a facing of terry towelling on the R.S. along the hem to catch any drips. Unfortunately this does not look attractive on raincoats and here the problem seems to be insoluble.

Processes

Preparing the pattern. Pin the paper pattern together along the fitting lines and try it on the wearer, or better still cut it out and tack up in muslin and adjust the fit and length to make absolutely sure that alterations on the garment will not be necessary when making it up in the actual fabric. All alterations will leave marks which cannot be removed.

Cutting out. Usually a paper pattern gives only half the pattern, which is then cut out in double fabric. It is neither easy nor accurate to cut these fabrics out double. Therefore duplicate the pattern pieces on spare paper so that the complete pattern can be laid out on the fabric and cut out singly.

Transferring the fitting lines. Tailor tacking is out of the question because it will perforate the fabric.

Use dressmaker's carbon paper placed between the pattern and the W.S. of the fabric. Pencil through the fitting lines to transfer them. Each pattern piece will have to be traced separately.

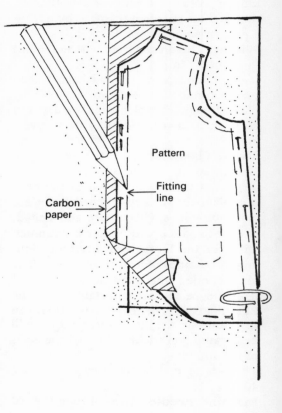

Pattern

Fitting line

Carbon paper

Assembling. Pin within the seam turnings or hold them together with paper clips or with masking tape.

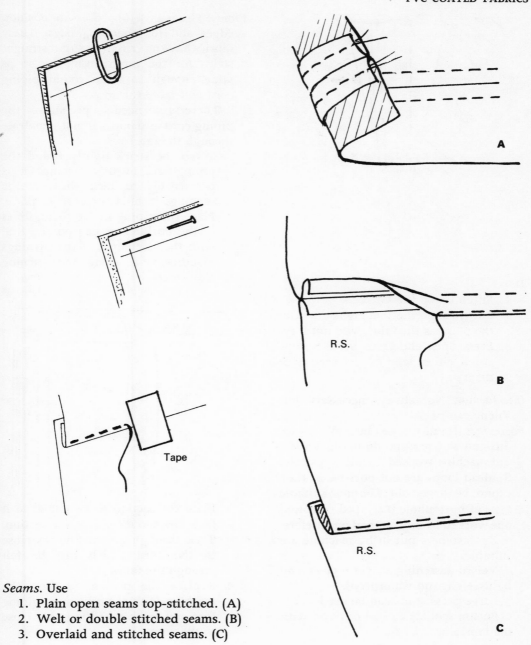

Tape

R.S.

R.S.

A

B

C

Seams. Use
  1. Plain open seams top-stitched. (A)
  2. Welt or double stitched seams. (B)
  3. Overlaid and stitched seams. (C)

95

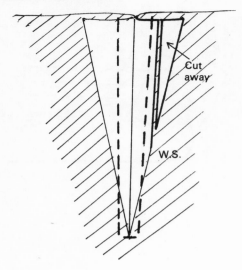

Darts

1. Stitch up on the W.S.
2. Cut through the fold right down to the point as the fabric will not fray.
3. Press open and from the R.S. top-stitch either side of the seam (see diagram).

Interfacings. Not always necessary but Vilene can be used.

Fastenings. Hand-worked buttonholes are difficult to work and do not look nice, but machine worked ones are possible. Rouleau loops are not possible as they cannot be turned out. The most suitable type of buttonhole is a piped or bound one worked by any method one prefers.

Zip fasteners put in by machine are suitable.

Velcro fastening is very good and lightweight and waterproof.

Large press studs can be used.

Button moulds can be covered with the fabric.

Piping. This is a useful process for cushion edges and for shopping bags. These fabrics have no crossway so cut straight strips for the piping. Cut the strips wide enough to wrap round piping cord and have turnings.

There is no need to pre-shrink the piping cord as damp will not penetrate through the fabrics.

1. Wrap the strips tightly round the piping and in this instance it is permissible to tack through the turnings to hold the cord in place.
2. Place the piping to the fitting lines of the cushion or bag on the R.S. with the raw edges of the turnings together. Pin along the turning allowance.

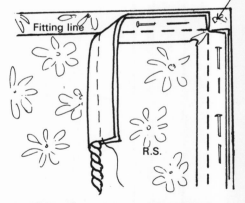

3. Place the section to be joined to it face down over the piped section. Tack through all thicknesses close to the cord which can be felt through the fabric.
4. Replace the presser foot on the machine with the zipper or piping foot and machine all together close to the cord.

Hems. Level the hem, using a chalk hem marker. Do not use pins.

The hem can be top-stitched from the R.S. to make it flat and decorative.

Another method is to fix it to the W.S. with adhesive.

In neither case can the hem be let down to conform with changes in fashion.

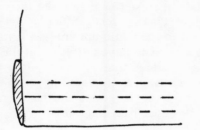

Linings. Tricel, taffeta and even quilted linings can be put into raincoats.
1. Make the lining up entirely.
2. Put the coat W.S. out on a dummy or hang it on a coat hanger.
3. Put the W.S. of the lining to the W.S. of the coat and pin the seams of the lining to the seam turnings of the coat. Take care not to put the pins right through the coat so that they make marks on the R.S.
4. Fold in the turnings all round the outside of the lining and pin through them, here and there, to hold them to the facings and hem of the garment. Hem the folded edges to the PVC fabric all round and then remove the pins from the seams.

Pressing

It is possible to press on the W.S. under dry muslin using a cool iron. If the iron is too hot the PVC coating will melt.

Aftercare

When the PVC fabric becomes soiled just wipe down with a damp cloth. If a garment is lined it can be washed so that the lining gets cleaned also.

CHECKED FABRICS

When fabrics have very tiny or sponge-bag types of check they can be treated as plain fabrics, but larger checks present cutting out and stitching up problems, as the pattern must be matched at the seams wherever possible.

Choosing styles

Avoid styles that are cut up into a lot of seams because this may make the matching of checks very difficult. Keep the seams to the minimum unless a feature of the style is to have parts cut on the cross to give added interest. Very often crossway cutting overcomes the problem of matching at the seams and making up is much easier (see diagram).

Buying the fabric

It is not wise to follow the pattern envelope slavishly for the amount of fabric to buy, because it does not cater for matching checks. Extra fabric will have to be bought for this. As a rough guide to this extra amount, calculate as follows: The pattern repeats down the length of the pattern, therefore measure the depth of one repeat. For a simple shift style when the back and the front are each cut in one pattern piece add the depth of one repeat to each piece, for example, depth of repeat = 15 cm (6 in.), add 30 cm (12 in.) to the amount of fabric stated on the pattern envelope and with long sleeves it may be necessary to add yet one more repeat, making it 45 cm (18 in.) in all. When the fabric is wide and the pattern pieces can be cut out side by side instead of one under the other, no extra fabric need be bought unless there are long sleeves which may need one repeat extra.

Remember that when the check is an uneven one use the amount stated on the pattern envelope for fabric *with nap* and then add the extra.

When buying fabric for pleated skirts the width of the repeat must be taken into account also and lengths of fabric may have to be joined so that when the fabric is pleated up the checks run in continuous sequence across it as though the pleats were not there. The depth of the pleat should be either half or the full width of a repeat, and in order to do this it may be necessary to buy an extra length of fabric, depending on how wide the fabric is.

Layout

Where there is an underarm dart the checks should match from the hem of the pattern piece upwards as far as the dart which will then throw the pattern out on the front bodice and it is less noticeable if the pattern does not match from the dart to the armhole than from the dart down to the waist or hem. Always match the fitting lines – never the outer edge of the turnings.

If there is a dominant stripe in the tartan type of check make sure that it is arranged to come straight down the centre front and back of a garment, because if it is off centre it will make the garment look unbalanced. Also this stripe should be arranged to come straight down the centre of each sleeve.

Watch where the balance marks of the bodice armhole lie on the checks and

arrange the corresponding balance marks of the sleeve on the same part of the pattern, so that the checks will match around the sleeve and across the front and back of the bodice (see diagram).

A tight-fitting sleeve with an elbow dart will throw the sleeve seam out from the dart to the wrist, but this is unavoidable.

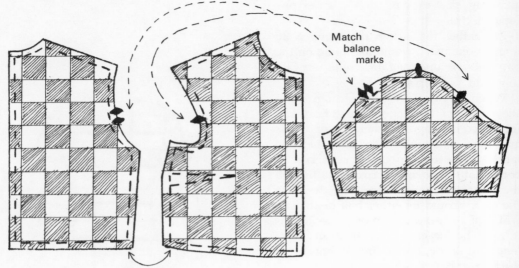

Match balance marks

Match here

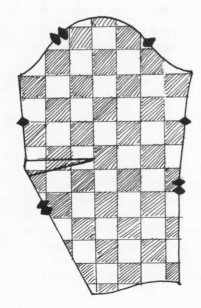

When the check is uneven the layout problem is greater and the layout given on a pattern instruction sheet for fabrics with nap should be followed. If the lines in the checks run, for example, thin – thick – medium, in that order across the fabric and down the length of it, the pattern pieces must be so placed that the sequence is maintained both ways on the garment. Watch that the back and front hem line are on identical parts of the check.

Diagram A shows the layout for a skirt cut on the cross and diagram B shows how, when it is put together, side and centre seams match.

Processes

Parts cut on the cross must be handled very carefully to prevent them from stretching and becoming distorted. Work on a large table and lay them flat and completely relaxed when tacking up.

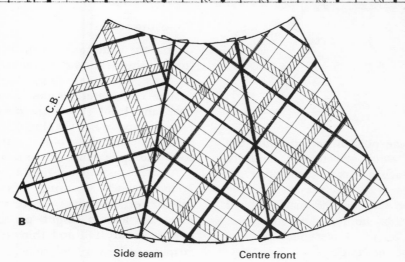

A

B

Side seam   Centre front

Seams. Plain or welt seams are the most suitable for these fabrics.

1. Pin seams together, matching the checks by turning first from one side to the other, and place the pins *across* the seam where the lines of the checks match. Use plenty of pins, particularly when the checks are irregular.
2. Tack up with *small* stitches, which are more likely to keep the pattern in place.
3. Remove the pins for fitting but replace them very carefully afterwards exactly at right angles to the fitting line.

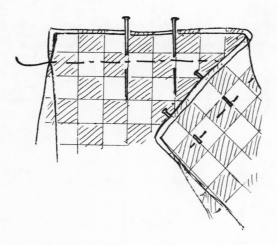

4. Keep the pins in and machine the seam taking the needle carefully over each pin as it is encountered. In this way the pressure of the presser foot on the machine will not push the top layer of fabric along on the lower one and disarrange the checks.

Curved plain seams and welt seams should be pinned in place and slip-tacked from the right side in order to keep the checks matched.

Hems. As most hems are curved it is not usually possible to turn the hem up along a line of checks, it must be levelled in the usual way and the checks will probably dip in the centre front and centre back.

STRIPED FABRICS

Stripes may be woven into a fabric, in which case they will definitely be on the straight grain or they may be printed on it and may be slightly off grain. In the latter case, if the fault is not very bad, cut with the stripes and sacrifice the grain but if it is really bad, return the fabric to the shop. The stripes may be vertical or horizontal, and even or uneven in colour or width.

Choosing styles

Unless one is designing with the stripes, turning them this way or the other or on the cross, the fewer seams there are in a design the better. Styles with centre back and front seams are possibly the best because waist shaping can be done in the seams thus avoiding darts which spoil the appearance of vertical stripes.

Always take your figure type into account when choosing this type of fabric. Vertical stripes can be very slimming and add to height, particularly if one is already tall and thin. Horizontal stripes can be very enlarging.

Layout

Symmetrical stripes are those arranged in such a sequence that whichever way pattern pieces are cut, the stripes will match up and such an example would be coloured stripes arranged red, white, blue, white and repeated in this order. Watch out for stripes which are not symmetrical, which may run as follows: red, white, blue and continue in this sequence. To understand this more clearly, paint both these stripe sequences on sheets of paper and, from them, cut out small dress pattern shapes (such as can be traced off the layout of a paper pattern instruction sheet). Play around with them to find out how the stripes will come together where seams have to be joined.

When a dress has no C B seam but buttons up down the front, vertical stripes must run all round the dress in the sequence in which they are arranged on the fabric, so all pattern pieces must be placed on the fabric the right way up as though it had a nap, and no pieces can be turned upside down for more economical cutting. Sometimes a dress is designed so that stripes which are not symmetrical are 'mirrored'. To understand this, paint three stripes on paper in this order, red, white, blue and hold the paper close to a mirror.

The stripes will reflect in the reverse order, namely, blue, white, red. A dress with mirrored stripes must have C F and C B seams and the layout is planned as follows: right front pattern piece is placed the right way up on the fabric, the left front upside down, the left back the right way up and the right back

upside down. Mirrored stripes can form a V at the seams when the fabric is cut on the cross. With a style like this quite a lot of fabric will be wasted in the cutting out and a longer length should be purchased than would otherwise be necessary.

When horizontal stripes are not symmetrical pattern pieces must not be turned upside down because the stripes will not match. The fabric has nap. When cutting pattern pieces out of double fabric, make sure that horizontal stripes lie exactly on top of each other. When stripes are vertical, watch the colour sequence, for example, if the stripes are blue, white, blue, white throughout, fold the fabric down the centre of either a blue or a white stripe so that one complete stripe will run down the centre of a garment, say a blue one with a white one equally either side of it. With the fabric folded in this way, the white stripes of the top layer will lie directly

103

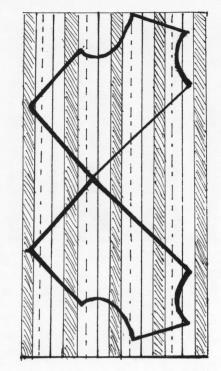

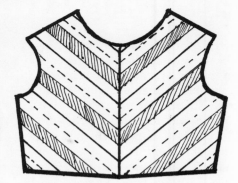

Non-symmetrical stripes cut on the cross

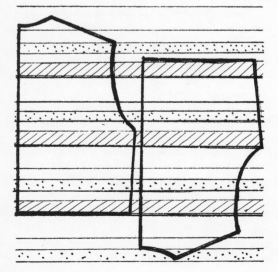

Incorrect layout of horizontal stripes

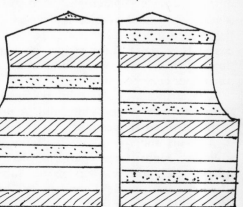

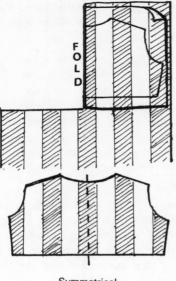

Symmetrical

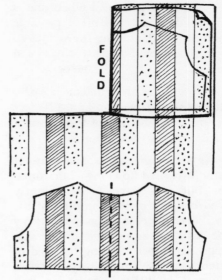

Not symmetrical

over the white stripes of the under layer and the blue over the blue. However, this is not quite the same when the stripes are not symmetrical, i.e. red, white, blue, etc. Choose the widest, or, if they are all equal, the stripe with the dominating colour and fold the fabric through the centre of this stripe, say the blue one, then the white stripe of the top layer will lie over the red one of the under layer. In this way the sequence is maintained and the dominating stripe comes down the centre.

Processes

Make the seams as described for checked fabrics, placing the pins across each stripe or, if it is a wide stripe, on either side of it, so that the stripes do not slip during the stitching.

Curved and difficult seams should always be slip-tacked from the R.S.

Pleats. These can be quite interesting because even-striped fabric can be pleated up so that all one colour shows on top and the other colour is revealed only when the pleats swing open.

Crossway cutting. Much play can be made with stripes cut directly on the cross and crossway strips can be used for binding or facing raw edges decoratively. When crossway fabric has to be joined, make sure that it is joined along a stripe. If the stripes are blue and white alternately, place a blue stripe over a white one and join the two strips together along the edges of the stripes so that when the fabric is opened out the sequence is maintained. This also applies to straight cut fabric

105

and is particularly useful when one is short of fabric, as it is often possible to piece it together along the stripes so that it will never show that it has been joined.

Patch pockets. These are much more easily applied if the stripes run in a different direction from the rest of the garment and this will also add interest.

Hems. As with checks, a hem cannot usually be turned up along a horizontal stripe but will have to be slightly curved because of the contours of the body. When there is a dominant heavy stripe it is an advantage if one can arrange for it to run along the fold of the hem, but this is not always possible because it is difficult to judge just where the hem is going to fall when cutting out, especially when the fabric is heavy and may drop when it has been hung up for a time.

Collars. These are easier to apply if the stripes run in a different direction from the garment, for example if the garment has vertical stripes those on the collar can run horizontally. Where this cannot happen, the stripes on the collar must be matched very carefully with those on the garment and the facing.

Fastenings. The only problem is when the stripes are irregular in width or colour and are horizontal. The space between each buttonhole should be such that each one lies on the same coloured stripe.

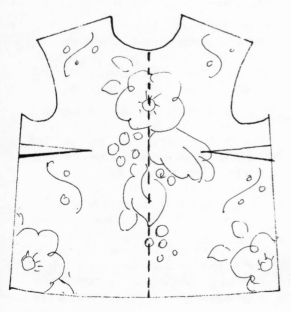

FABRICS WITH A LARGE MOTIF

Choosing a style

Do not choose a pattern with a lot of seams which will cut up the large motif and make it look a muddle. Keep everything simple and let the fabric make the dress. Extra fabric may be needed to match the pattern.

Layout

Study the fabric carefully because there is often an 'up and a down' and then the pattern pieces have to be placed all the same way up. Always arrange the pattern pieces so that the dominant motif comes right down the centre of a dress and avoid large areas of pattern coming either side on the chest. Make sure that large areas of pattern come on the same level on the back and front sections of the dress so that they do not look as though they have slipped down in places.

The problems lie mainly with the layout and careful placing of the pattern and then the making up is quite straightforward.

20. Miscellaneous fabrics

The fabrics included in this chapter are those with only one or two special problems.

LINEN

Used for dresses and skirts.

Problems

1. The fabrics fray badly when cut. Allow wider than usual turnings and cut out with pinking shears. Trim the turnings later when they have to be neatened. The neatening can be hand overcasting or machine zig-zag.
2. Pressing can leave shiny imprints on the R.S. Press seams carefully on the W.S. over a roller and, if necessary, place brown paper between the seam turnings and the garment before pressing.
3. The fabric has a natural sheen and whichever side is touched by the iron acquires the sheen, so that if a matt surface is required on the R.S., press the fabric on the W.S. and vice versa. Use a hot iron.
4. Try to avoid repeatedly pressing the edges of pleats heavily as creases constantly pressed in the same place cause the fibres to crack along the folds in the course of time.

GROSGRAIN

Width. 91 cm (36 in.) or as a ribbon in various widths. This is a fabric with a heavy horizontal rib.
Sewing thread. Mercerised cotton size 40.
Hand-sewing needle. Size 8 sharps.
Machine needle. 14 English or 80 Continental.
Stitch length. 10–12 stiches per 2·5 cm (1 in.). 2–2½ setting on a Continental machine.
Interfacing. Organdie, adhesive staflex or a nonwoven interfacing.
Underlining. Not necessary.
Lining. Taffeta.
Hems.

1. Hems require to be turned up carefully. Stiffen them with horsehair braid.
2. Tack in the hem level.
3. Place the horsehair braid in position on the W.S. so that 6 mm ($\frac{1}{4}$ in.) lies below the hem level tacking line and the braid lies on the garment.
4. Catch stitch the lower edge of the braid to the hem turning.
5. Trim the hem turning to the required depth and neaten the raw edge by hand overcasting or machine zig-zag.
6. Turn the hem up along the level line and tack through all thicknesses 6 mm ($\frac{1}{4}$ in.) above the folded edge.

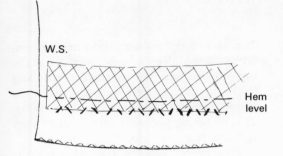

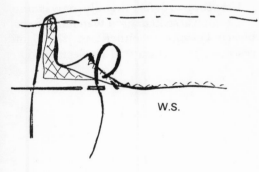

Take every precaution to prevent a shiny imprint on the R.S.

Avoid getting any moisture near it as the fabric spots very easily and these watermarks are almost impossible to get out. Do not wear the garment in the rain.
Cleaning. Always dry clean.

FACE CLOTH

This is a heavy woollen fabric used for coats. It has a fine pile nap on the R.S. giving a slight velvet effect. Because of this all pattern pieces must be laid in one direction only so that the nap smooths downwards, otherwise shading takes place.

The fabric is easy to stitch up but poor pressing can cause shiny impressions of tackings and turnings on the R.S. Therefore press on the W.S. under a damp cloth and avoid pressing over tacking; in fact it is better to remove all possible tacking before pressing.

Press all seams over a roller with brown paper between the turnings and the garment.

As the fabric is rather bulky, thin out seams and turnings as far as possible. If turnings should leave a shiny impression after pressing this can be removed if the fabric is held for a few moments in the steam of a boiling kettle.

FELT

This is a heavy non-woven fabric made by matting and fusing fibres together into a dense mass and is sometimes in fashion for skirts, boleros and caps.

7. Slip-hem the hem edge in place very lightly, leaving the thread as slack as possible.
8. Remove all tacking *before* pressing the bottom edge with the flat of the hand. Avoid using an iron if possible.

Pressing is the main difficulty with this fabric. Always press *lightly* on the W.S. *dry*.

Press all seams over a roller.

Never press over tacking as this will leave marks that are difficult to remove.

The fabric stretches round curves, such as necks. This can be prevented by making rows of decorative machine stitching around the curve or by invisibly hemming 6 mm ($\frac{1}{4}$ in.) tape on the W.S.

The feed of the sewing machine can mark the fabric, so always place tissue paper between the feed and the fabric when stitching.

The needle makes punctures in the fabric, so use a fine machine needle and a long machine stitch, 8 per 2·5 cm (1 in.). Avoid having to unpick.

Felted fabric is not so strong as woven fabric so do not expect hard wear from it.

Felt has no elasticity and will not drape and is suitable only for simple styles such as waistcoats and slightly flared skirts.

WINCEYETTE

This is a cheap cotton fabric used extensively for children's nightwear. It has the top surface brushed to make it soft and fluffy so that air can be trapped in the fibres to make the fabric warm to wear. This brushing process causes it to be very inflammable.

Winceyette can be treated with the Proban process to make it flame resistant and washing instructions are usually given to customers when they buy this fabric. These should not be disregarded.

Use soapless detergent only for washing.

Do not use soap in hard water and *do not* bleach because in either case the flame resistant protection will be destroyed.

Index